Clayfeld Rejoices,

Clayfeld Laments

Books of Poetry and Criticism
by Robert Pack:

AFFIRMING LIMITS:
Essays on Mortality, Choice, and Poetic Form

FACES IN A SINGLE TREE:
A Cycle of Monologues

WAKING TO MY NAME:
New and Selected Poems

KEEPING WATCH

NOTHING BUT LIGHT

HOME FROM THE CEMETERY

GUARDED BY WOMEN

A STRANGER'S PRIVILEGE

WALLACE STEVENS:
An Approach to His Poetry and Thought

THE IRONY OF JOY

Clayfeld Rejoices, Clayfeld Laments

A SEQUENCE OF POEMS

by Robert Pack

DAVID R. GODINE

Publisher · Boston

The author wishes to thank the editors of the following magazines and anthologies in which most of these poems first appeared: *The American Scholar, Antæus, Black Warrior Magazine, The Bread Loaf Anthology, The Denver Quarterly, The Georgia Review, The Kenyon Review, The New England Review, The New Republic, The Paris Review, Poetry Magazine, Poetry Miscellany, Poetry Northwest, Prairie Schooner, Quarterly West, Tendril Magazine,* and *The Webster Review.*

To Patty, Erik, Pamela, and Kevin for cheering Clayfeld on in the morning, and to John Bertolini, John Elder, Jay Parini, and Gary Margolis for reassuring Clayfeld's narrator toward nightfall.

First edition published in 1987 by
David R. Godine, Publisher, Inc.
Horticultural Hall
300 Massachusetts Avenue
Boston, Massachusetts 02115

Library of Congress Cataloging in Publication Data
Pack, Robert, 1929–
    Clayfeld rejoices, Clayfeld laments.
    I. Title.
PS3566.A28C54   1987   811'.54   87-7414
ISBN 0-87923-695-7
ISBN 0-87923-696-5 (pbk.)

First edition
Printed in the United States of America

Contents

Clayfeld Rejoices,

Clayfeld Laments

/ Narrator's Prologue

When April rains release the frozen roots,
Swelling the soil beneath the suck of boots,
And dewy crocuses and daffodils
Spill out their colors as the locked stream spills
Over awakened stones down to the lake
Where willows flash their first buds at the break
Of chickadee-melodic dawn, there starts
A quickened longing in all human hearts —
"For what? For travel to some choicer place?
New knowledge? Or a dream-familiar face?"
Clayfeld, at odds with impulses like this,
Prefers to stay at home. He blows a kiss
To transcendental yearnings in the breeze,
Surveys bent birches, ice-cracked apple trees,
Declaims: "This is the wrong time of the year
To take a trip, too much needs tending here!"
The trees should have been pruned a month ago;
The woodshed sags from its long load of snow;
A porcupine has chewed the handles of
His garden spade, his hoe and rake, in love
With salt rubbed in from human sweat. The fault
Is grave that Clayfeld shares this taste for salt —
(The thieving porcupine had to be shot) —
His palate pleads for pleasures spicy hot,
Sin's wages measured in cholesterol,
Which later I'll enumerate in full,
Assuming my profane, plump Muse allows;
I'll skim creamed Clayfeld's loves from sacred cows.
As Clayfeld's narrator, I might as well
Milk dry the tales I am bemused to tell
To squeeze a bucket's laughter in your lives,
By showing you, fit reader, love survives
Repeated failure and repeated loss.
With spirit streaming through his body's dross,

Clayfeld's foul-ups are typical: you'll see
Yourself in him, surmising him in me;
Scapegoat and friend and representative —
There's no vice in him virtue can't forgive.
Spared by mere chance from accident and war,
But not the salty wounds of love, that's sure,
Clayfeld finds something in his flesh that sings
Itself anew despite his sufferings,
Some lucky gift for stubborn happiness —
A blessing if one thinks laughter can bless.

    No history to call my own, I need
To cultivate in emptiness — a seed,
A storytelling pulsing poem-song
To sow the mind and thump the heart along
Its immemorial, iambic way,
Still harvesting what roots of words can say,
With rhymes to measure how our bodies go
Like rabbit footprints pausing in the snow.
I need a fabled heritage to live
A while, as long as books are read to give
Companionship, each one of us alone
In one collective fate of flesh and bone.

    My role is feigning witness to Clayfeld —
As if his life were lived to be beheld,
Although, had I a story of my own,
He might have been my father or my son;
I might have eased him when he needed me,
Held him, assured him and . . . but let that be.
Yet, maybe I can help him, like a friend,
Unpacking his heart's burden at the end.

    Fly to your readers, larkful songs, and say
You sentence them to tears poems weep away,
The laughter worded-seeing adds to sight —
A fleeting touch of Clayfeld in the night.

/ Clayfeld's Microscope

Clayfeld recalls his hobby as a boy:
     cultivating protozoa
in water taken from the tadpole pond
     behind the barn.
Peering through his birthday microscope,
     he watches an amoeba
plump out its pseudopod, engulf some algae,
     meditate a moment,
then constricting in the middle
     by sheer force of will,
just pull apart, tearing in two its body,
     nucleus and all.
Once Clayfeld sat for five hours straight
     to see how many times
the first amoeba would divide, straining
     not to lose sight of it.
He named her Mom so he could follow her
     among the swarming
paramecia, euglena, dead specks,
     and bits of stone.
A problem there, of course, since once
     Mom had divided,
which one then was Mom? "How can you tell?"
     Clayfeld's twin brother asked,
yet Clayfeld had the spooky sense
     somehow he knew—
something about the way Mom moved,
     some fluid ease,
enabled him to choose which one she was.
     Clayfeld was not as certain
of the girls at school. It puzzled him
     to find how rapidly
his feelings changed, how none of them
     attracted him for long,

though he'd still tighten in his pants
    when they were giggling
in the library, or when they
    globbed together
in the cafeteria. One day,
    sitting with them
during lunch, Mima, the girl he liked
    about a month ago,
stuffed both her cheeks with gooey bread,
    puckered her lips,
and blew a slimy kiss at him. But something
    crazy happened when
he squinted back his eyes: he saw
    her face as if she were
a huge amoeba, her dark mouth its nucleus,
    the instant it divides,
and screamed at her, "Don't do that, Mom!"
    Their laughter made him blush
so hard he burst into another of his
    periodic nosebleeds;
they had to lead him, wadded napkins
    covering his cheeks,
to get an ice pack from the skinny nurse:
    "Old Bones will save you!"
taunted through the corridors. Clayfeld
    got Mima pregnant when he
turned eighteen. Through the cold night before
    they went to the abortionist,
with money borrowed from his older sister,
    they made such compulsive love
beside the dry stone wall his father built
    to frame the barn that they amazed
themselves. Their bodies seemed beyond whatever words
    might bring them back to who they were.

"Look at the stars; I've never seen so many
        scattered stars!" was all
Clayfeld could say. Mima wept to herself
        as dawn stirred in the pines.
"I'm sorry for us all," he thought she murmured,
        swearing that he'd marry her
when they were old enough to keep a child.
        Morosely kissing her good-bye
before she climbed the ramp to fly to college
        in the west, Clayfeld did not admit
as their lips parted that he felt relieved.
        For one whole week he stared
into his microscope, but when a cell
        divided, Clayfeld now could not
distinguish which one was the one
        he started with, and when
the time arrived for him to go, he left a note
        that turned his ordinary
microscope into a gift he hoped
        his brother might enjoy:
"For me it's been like studying the universe."
        At school his interests changed to how
the earth evolved; Clayfeld became a sculptor
        when his gloom got worse.

/ *Clayfeld's Duck*

Clayfeld's father died after two strokes
        when Clayfeld was fifteen.
His last words were: "Take care of Buff,"
        but Clayfeld didn't know

anyone named Buff, and wondered
	whether Buff might have been
his father's dog when he was young. His mother,
	one year later, married Bill,
so all of them moved north to Maine,
	making the cattle farm their home
where Bill's pa had been born. Bill bought some ducks,
	plump, luminescent white
with orange bills, and Clayfeld kept them
	in the unused chicken coop
that he repaired. Six eggs appeared;
	Clayfeld inspected them
each morning when he did his chores,
	freshening the water for his ducks,
bringing them their grain. One night a weasel
	broke into their pen;
when Clayfeld found them, feathers fluttered
	in the dusty air, although
they had survived, quivering together
	in the corner of their hutch.
The eggs were shattered—all but one
	which had a jagged crack-line
like a pumpkin's grin. As Clayfeld poked it
	gently in the gusting dawn,
a head popped out as if it were a toy,
	and Clayfeld jumped,
gashing his head against the gate.
	Some birds know who their mother is
because mother means the first thing moving
	that her baby sees; and, yes,
you've guessed it, that's what Clayfeld was:
	fate had inscrutably decreed
that Clayfeld would become a mother duck.
	Ishmael scuttled after him,

as ducks always have done, and squawked
    if Clayfeld walked too far ahead.
At dinnertime, Clayfeld would put him
    in the pocket of his shirt
against his chest and let him snuggle in.
    His sister scolded him
for interfering with the course of things,
    and yet she helped him build a box,
set with a bulb, to warm his duck at night.
    Bill lost his hand
trying to fix a combine in the field,
    and carried it a hundred yards,
wrapped tightly in his shirt, back to the house.
    When Ishmael was full grown,
Clayfeld released him on the lake
    to join the other ducks
as maple leaves were falling and red squirrels
    rasped at each other
in the chill of sharpened light. In June
    Clayfeld returned from school,
and there was Ishmael in the lake as if
    awaiting him. Clayfeld hooted,
flapping his arms, but Ishmael would not
    come to him, coasting along
the hazy water's farthest edge.
    Bill had been fitted
with a plastic hand, and Clayfeld was surprised
    that he could cut his food
or pull the trigger of his gun, but when
    his mother pressed it to her lips
to show how proud she was of Bill,
    the shattered eggs, the hunch-backed weasel
still surveying them, flashed in his mind.
    For one whole month Clayfeld

glutted himself with food, or sitting silent
    on the limestone ledge, he'd watch
the ducks paddling around the lily pads.
    Bill kneeled beside him,
resting his plastic hand on Clayfeld's arm;
    "Isn't that Ishmael," Bill asked,
"the third one in formation by the cove?
    A stranger couldn't tell him from the rest."
Clayfeld surprised himself to hear what words
    leaped out of him: "Ishmael's the one
beyond that bank of stones," he said, knowing
    a grove of birches was reflected
in the water there, reflecting in the sun.

/ Clayfeld's Glove

Clayfeld believed indulging in one's whims
    improved the circulation
of despondent blood; whims, the sculptor in him
    could persuade himself,
counted as a form of inspiration.
    One day, browsing
in a sports equipment store, he noticed how
    the baseball gloves had changed,
how large the webbing had become, and he decided
    he would fly to Arizona,
where his mother lived, to see if she had stored
    the yellow baseball glove
Clayfeld had oiled and pounded into shape
    when he was still a boy.

"Are you all right?" the salesman asked,
    and Clayfeld knew
he must have blushed to recollect the time
    he'd grabbed his baseball glove
to hide his private parts that night
    his mother, without warning,
walked into his room. He thought maybe he'd sculpt
    a naked statue of himself—
a true artistic first: a baseball glove where once
    a fig leaf would have been.
Clayfeld awoke in Arizona to the smell
    of lamb chops sizzling,
which his mother served him with his eggs,
    just as she used to do
when he was lifting weights to put some muscle
    on his skinny frame.
"Everything I've kept of yours," she said,
    "is packed away in boxes
chronologically and stacked in the garage."
    Shoes, hair clippings, letters,
layer after layer, like excavations
    from an ancient Jericho,
waited to be exhumed. And then, behold!
    he found a baseball glove,
but one too skimpy to have been his own.
    Maybe, he thought, this was
his father's glove; maybe Mother had mistaken
    Father's glove for his?
Another statue he might sculpt appeared
    in Clayfeld's mind: his father, poised
in naked grandeur, just as Michelangelo
    had once conceived his David,
slingshot stone in hand, prepared to backhand
    any well-hit grounder

that might yield the rally-killing double play.
    "I don't know how
this glove could be your father's,"
    Clayfeld's mother scolded him,
and then it all came swirling back to her:
    "You couldn't have been more
than four or five," she said, "that spring your father
    took you out to have a catch
when he had finished with his chores — and I
    mean every single day!
I'd stand there in the doorway shouting
    'Dinner will get spoiled
unless the two of you come in right now!'
    but nothing I could threaten
seemed to do much good. And so one evening
    after you had muddied up
the living room as usual, I boiled the glove,
    piled mashed potatoes
neatly in the pocket, sprinkled it
    with parsley, squeezed into
my tightest bathing suit, my highest heels,
    and sashayed in
to score my point." A statue of his mother
    formed in Clayfeld's mind,
and then Clayfeld recalled his father's words
    before he tucked him
into bed that night: "From now on, Son,
    we'll have to end
our catch on time." It had begun to rain.
    He saw the red buds
of the maple tree outside his room
    begin to sway and swell.
His father handed him a sandwich
    he had sneaked upstairs

inside his baseball cap. "I'll bet you didn't know
  that I could cook," he said.
Now in this Arizona noon, those open boxes
  blazing in the entryway
of the garage, the lines in Clayfeld's mother's face
  seemed smoothed out by the sun.
"Yes, everything will be put back exactly
  in its place," he promised her.
But Clayfeld wondered if his grief would ever end.
  Maybe if he had children
of his own? He thought someday he'd do
  his father's bust — he'd catch the grim
thrust of his head, like David looking past his shoulder
  through the empty light,
without his body there to trouble him.

/ Clayfeld Amused

Clayfeld had long forgotten playing "doctor"
  with his older sister, Melly,
on the languid days at home from school when both
  of them were sick — how they took turns
with his toy stethoscope, examining
  each other's parts, seeking a clue
for the right cure, though titillated Clayfeld
  never knew if Melly, nicknamed
from Melpomene, played "doctor" with his brother, too.
  The shiver in his chest
when she was stitching up his cowboy wounds
  returned — as if his flesh recalled —

that noon his sister, married now, stopped by
  his studio to spend the day.
"Just following an impulse!" Melly greeted him.
  Clayfeld complained he couldn't get
the statue he was working on exactly right:
  a naked Indian girl,
carrying a basket piled with gleaming fruit.
  "I'll model her for you!"
asserted Melly, stripping to her waist
  before he could decline, and then
she struck a pose of offering some grapes.
  Clayfeld continued texturing
the surface of a peach to dull the sheen,
  but Melly's breasts distracted him;
superbly round, the left was larger, he could see,
  than its less ripened twin,
and, drooping lower, marred her body's symmetry.
  Yet should he, Clayfeld wondered,
balance them—an artful compromise—lift up
  the left a bit and add some volume
to the right? Why so? The human form is not
  symmetrical—the male's left
testical, his brother once had chuckled to observe,
  hangs lower than the right;
a triple helix of two veins, one artery—
  the cord, *umbilicus*,
coils counter-clockwise from the fetus to
  the providential mother source.
"O Muse made manifest in breasts askew,
  are you at last revealed
incarnate unto me?" asked Clayfeld's awe-struck voice;
  then, chisel brandished in the air,
catching the dusty window-light behind his back,
  he gave shape to the girl

by imitating Melly's breasts right there
    before his eyes — although he felt
compelled, it's true, to rearrange an apple
    and a pomegranate, weight
for compensating weight, upon the right side
    of the cherry-laden basket.
"Yes, I will leave Jim," his sister blurted out;
    "we've stayed together for the sake
of having someone there to blame for love
    each of us lacks. This pattern
of attack and then remorse has got to break."
    Inspired on the spot, Clayfeld
retorted that all physicists once trusted
    in the law of parity —
nature revealed no bias left or right —
    but Madame Wu's experiment
proved that a cobalt-sixty nucleus would fling
    more magnetized electrons from
its south end than its north, as if on God's Creation Day
    He had decreed deep purpose
in contriving an exception to His tidy,
    ambidextrous cosmos for each
(strewn throughout His galaxies) lost one of us:
    Let south be found by following
electrons from my cobalt-sixty nucleus!
    Yet look into the quantum mess
of particles: causality, like human vows,
    degenerates to randomness.
"You're mimicking our brother," Melly said.
    "I know the two of you believe
I blundered into fruitless marriage on a whim;
    I also know why you're afraid
to show you care, why you're too strict in sculpting me.
    I may decide true love requires

that I have even breasts; if so," she winked,
    "I'll try cosmetic surgery."

/ Landscape Without Figures

    His father is not here to see
Clayfeld is absent from his painted scene.
    Only the slow cows graze
the clover field ascending to the ridge
    of forest pines, and stark
behind their silhouetted tips,
    the mountain range spreads out
its purple shade from north to south
    with intermittent sun
beneath the thickening low clouds
    whose upper edges flare
like ocean spray. If he were here, his father
    might have mused:
we'll have a thunderstorm this afternoon;
    his mother might have seen him
pause to watch a puddle where a hundred
    sulfur butterflies,
all bunching wing to wing, would swarm
    as if the streaking light
had fractured into momentary bits; she might
    have seen him taking down
the dead elms at the border of the field,
    and then pass on to spare
a rotted beech the pileated woodpecker
    had hollowed into home.

The flowing field does not reveal they're gone,
     how long ago or why
they left, but one can see the piled stone wall,
     descending to the bottom
of the picture frame that they had built
     to mark the plot they hoped
their son would want to make his own.
     And there's the stream they dammed
into a crawfish pond; and there, within the moist shade
     of the great white oak,
they gathered mushrooms in the misty fall.
     One cannot tell by looking
at the scene itself if he was right
     about the thunderstorm
so that the cows lay their bulks down beside
     the muddy water hole,
or if a slant wind split the hollowed tree,
     or if their son returned
with his own wife to build a house where they
     had portioned out the land
with stones collected from the field;
     for all those images
are solely what the eye can see—reduced
     by what Clayfeld has chosen
that his canvas should forget. There are
     no people here, only
his withdrawn hand, trained to paint out regret
     with disembodied love
of line and form. And yet Clayfeld is pleased
     he stressed the purple
of the mountain peaks, the woodpecker's red crest,
     the sun's reflected yellow
on the butterflies—they gather in a circle
     someone's wandering thoughts

might focus on. And Clayfeld tells the wife
     he has not met: "Though you can't
find me in this bright, abandoned scene,
     you'd know I lived here too,
touched by the pine scent of the wind; whoever
     you may be, my love, my father
would have sensed I painted this for you."

/ Clayfeld's Narrator Admires Clayfeld's Bridge

     Clayfeld's melancholy mood
invited him to watch the sinking sun
     repeat its orange fire
by blazing one by one upon the lily pads
     beneath the wooden bridge
that arched across the pond between
     the stiffened cattails
and the leaning reeds. And as the sun descended
     past the waving willow row,
Clayfeld could see—as he had seen for years—
     the streaked-gray cedar railing
sparkle momentary yellow from the breezy light
     reflected off the leaves
before the warm planks, whispering
     forgotten footfalls,
blurred through shades of purple into blue.
     From where he placed himself
on what he once had named his *vista throne*—
     a giant fallen oak
that crossed the stream source of the pond
     down at its turbid end—

Clayfeld could *not* see where the path
    beyond the house led
to the bridge, and, likewise, shrubbery concealed
    the narrowed pathway, winding
toward the mountain on the other side.
    The bridge, as Clayfeld wished it,
seemed to hover in the amber air,
    as if detached
from any recollection but the scene itself,
    as if Clayfeld were not
included there except that someone had to say:
    "The way the bridge's arc
completes the motif of the lily pads
    does not require a viewer here."
The night was almost settled in the pond by then;
    against a blotch of sky,
now underwater blue and roughly framed
    by hunching willow trees,
the bridge shone like a crescent silhouette
    some hand had penciled in,
connecting darkness on the house side
    of the pond to darkness
on the other where the mountain's shadows spread out
    when the moon was full.
This scene was so familiar to his summertime routine
    that Clayfeld could describe it
to himself no matter where he was; but now, released
    in easeful observation,
he beheld a figure enter from the right, pause
    at the center of the bridge
to watch the scattered lily flowers while
    they still floated in
a remnant of their glow, and then walk on
    to vanish where the rushes

ushered him away. His father, Clayfeld thought,
    had walked those boards
the night he was conceived and every night
    thereafter for about two months
until the pregnancy had been confirmed—
    according to his mother's story,
which she told him after Clayfeld's father died.
    Clayfeld emphatically
did not believe in ghosts, nor had his mother
    strolled out for a breath
that humid night; and he was certain he
    had not hallucinated
from his long-accustomed gloom the figure
    on the bridge. So he assumed
what he had seen, though not his father's spirit,
    actually was there—
a wave of shadows, cast by some configuration
    of the swaying bushes
and the gusted willow trees upon the pond
    and on the sleek round lily pads,
which were in turn projected on the bridge.
    Yet when I visited the farm
and sat on Clayfeld's giant oak, watching his bridge
    reflect the changing colors
of the lily pond, to see what shadows
    gathered in the dark,
the only image I could make appear—
    since no one crossed the bridge—
was Clayfeld waiting there exactly where I sat;
    I felt that I could feel
the melancholy in the delicately misted air
    that Clayfeld must have felt.
Yes, Clayfeld must have realized his life
    demanded that he seek

his heedlessly departing father in himself,
      although the one thing only
that—while pausing there by his old empty bridge
      and its viridian, reflecting
lily pads below—he felt he wholly knew
      was *they were beautiful*
all darkening before his eyes to blue.

/ *Clayfeld's Madonna*

October once again, and O, Clayfeld sees
      frantic yellow cedar waxwings
ravaging the clustered orange berries
      of the mountain ash.
Sitting on his old, oak stump, Clayfeld watches
      as the mist, lugubriously blue,
shades into purple in the valley reeds;
      and then fanfare of brazen
trumpet wind along the flaming sumac row
      reminds his meditating eyes
the sunset glow of maple red is all
      the meaning his life needs.
An unpicked apple focuses the evening
      to a final spark,
and Clayfeld peers across the valley
      down the Leonardo dark.
He strains to see—beyond the orchard slope,
      beyond the outcropped hill—
inside a cave where jagged shade rips farther back
      into more jagged shade until,

as if there were an entrance out the other way,
    a green shine glistens tiny
in the distance like an undiscovered bay.
    A table in the foreground,
set for three, shimmers in candlelight;
    a large bone-handled knife
beside an unsliced loaf of bread repeats
    the candle in its blade;
a fur-caped woman, reading to her child,
    lowers her book in her blue shade.
The chair across from hers, beside her son,
    stands empty as she cuts the bread,
when, at a noise, she looks beyond the cave,
    out through the valley blur,
where startled Clayfeld on his stump
    tenses, still watching her.
He thinks he can make out the sound
    that shaped the roundness
of her lips. An O, a lingering, expanding O,
    held even as the cave
begins to close. What does she call out in the night
    as her child's silver cup,
suspended in the candle's amber air,
    reflects the sliver of the moon
and penetrates the writhing shadows there?
    As the cave shuts, the candlelight
explodes its gasped intake of breath,
    piercing dazed Clayfeld's eyes
like a doomed star collapsing in its death.
    Clayfeld wraps his stiff arms
around himself against the chilling dew
    and stares, relieved,
into the imageless, familiar dark,
    though he still sees her face—

her straight, thin nose, her olive hue.
  Upon his stump, Clayfeld decides
he will outwait all sleep, listening still
  for fox cries and the last owl croon
until the dawn restores their colors to the leaves
  and drains the glimmer from the moon.
Warm reds! Clayfeld adores wild dogwood reds,
  euonymus, and firethorn
pyrocantha berries crowded into rows,
  and orange-red would be enough—
though only what a season's end bestows—
  if Clayfeld could believe
that droning O upon her lips moaned out for him.
  Perhaps the valley-echoes
warped the sound she made; perhaps she called
  his uncompleted name—
his nasal vowel baying in her throat, receding
  back into the letter "A"?

/ Clayfeld's Dream

Clayfeld was thirty when he started
  to record his dreams,
hoping for insight into why he fell
  in love with women
who did not return his love.
  He kept his dream-book
and an orange by his bed; waking, he'd sniff
  the orange, quarter it,
bite so his teeth would scrape against the pulpy white
  inside the peel, and let

his dream flow out revealed upon the page.
  Wearing his baseball cap,
he crouches on a stone outcropping
  of a cliff, obscured
by gusts of fog, unable to climb down;
  he hears a sudden cry
that seems to echo from a winding cave,
  and then a taloned bird,
something like a pterodactyl,
  swoops on him, hooks him
by his flailing legs, and flies off,
  dangling him across the sea.
Clayfeld can feel the rhythm of its wings
  thrumming the air,
almost as if he soars by his own will;
  but as he spreads his arms
the bird releases him, and, falling slowly,
  waving his baseball cap,
helpless Clayfeld drops into the sea.
  When Clayfeld has the dream again,
he watches it inside a movie house,
  and when apparently
the dream ends with a thudding splash,
  the theater lights abruptly
are turned on, and there before the empty screen,
  ruler in hand, stands
Clayfeld's kindergarten teacher, ordering
  silence in the room;
then, pointing to the row where gabbing Maralyn
  pulls at her braid as if
it were a beard, she asks if Clayfeld drowns.
  Maralyn folds her arms
over her face — only her nose peeks through —
  and will not answer her.

When Clayfeld actually awakes, he thinks
    at first (because his dream
was just recalled within his dream) it has
    already been recorded
in his diary, but when he tries to write
    the whole dream down, knowing
something fateful at the end is missing,
    Maralyn has disappeared.
Clayfeld sucks his orange, spitting seeds
    into his hand, but all
that he can picture is her empty seat;
    as sunlight blazing
white in spindrift as the wind, without direction,
    swirls over the stirred sea.
About a year had passed since Clayfeld
    started his dream diary
when Clayfeld met a girl one summer sunrise
    on a solitary beach.
Black hair framed Maralyn's pale olive skin,
    and she allowed Clayfeld
to sit by her, but when he muses how we cling
    to "sunrise," obsolete
though that word is, as if we'd never learned
    the tilt and spin of earth,
she brandishes an orange from her purse
    and, grinning, orbits it
from ear to ear around his planetary head.
    That instant, dazzled Clayfeld
falls in love with her — takes her free, earthbound hand,
    proposes on the spot.
"Say, Yes," he hears himself blurt out,
    "before you tell me anything
about yourself!" Still turning the bright orange
    in the risen light, Maralyn

replies: "I'll marry when I overcome
my fear of emptiness—
stars hurtling outward and away, creating space
with nothing there."
"The heaviest rejection I've received,"
Clayfeld observed,
yet he decided to record the story
of his meeting Maralyn
as just another entry in his diary,
though strictly speaking,
he well knew, one could not classify it
as a dream. Fate intervened
one summer later, when a girl named Marylyn
(spelled with a middle *y*)
accepted Clayfeld after she had read his diary.
"Coincidence!" she said,
"Marriages are not conceived in dreams;
they are invented
by a vow to keep a vow!" Heavy again,
though Clayfeld was delighted
to agree, he felt relief watching those words
straighten her lip-line,
square her jaw, and by next morning
Clayfeld was convinced
her grim expression freed him finally
from his obsessive dream.
And yet his diary's last entry tells
of one dream more: of Maralyn
emerging from the sea, spume at her breasts,
spray frothing on her face,
though Clayfeld saw, without a doubt, her face
was *his*. He married Marylyn,
but later got divorced, wearing his baseball cap
the rainy day they signed

the legal settlement. His sorrow seems
    implied by all the orange stains
that look like sunsets on the cliffs, or passing birds,
    in Clayfeld's diary of dreams.

/ Clayfeld Takes Another Chance

Soon after his divorce, Clayfeld, childless,
    and also wifeless now,
retreating from his gloom, flew to Las Vegas
    to woo Lady Luck, telling himself
he'd either make a fortune or he'd lose
    the last buck he had stashed away—
if that were in the stars. Blackjack was his best game,
    but when he saw those one-armed bandits
lined up, glittering like urinals,
    he filled his pockets
with a stack of shiny silver dollars
    and, high-spirited, began to play,
pulling the handle down at intervals
    precisely timed
to cast a spell on the machine. It seemed
    to have a tendency
to turn up cherries on the left, oranges
    in the middle slot, then lemons
on the right. "Concentrate on cherries,"
    cool Clayfeld told himself,
recalling Grandpa's cherry trees in June
    curving across the hill in rows,
and Grandma asking if her pie was tart enough.
    Clayfeld lost track of how much

he had spent, and then, meticulous as planets
    wheeling in their course,
the one-armed bandit click-clicked into place
    three neatly drawn vaginas,
darkly luminous as lemon moons. A joke!
    of course this was a joke,
and yet where was the splash of spilling coins
    for three vaginas of a kind —
a winning combination, he was sure;
    a pretty cheap joke, Clayfeld thought.
"Don't touch this damn machine till I get back!"
    Clayfeld's command barked out
to no one in particular, huffing away
    to get the manager, Ms. Minters,
but when they returned, only two lemons
    and an orange stared at them.
"I'm sorry, sir," she said, "I can assure you
    we have never used vaginas
here in our machines." Some underworld conspiracy
    has been misplaced, thought Clayfeld.
Still, I know enough to guess that he invented
    the vaginas — no, not to deceive
himself, or me, but to replace what's missing
    in his life (maybe the child that he
and Mima, and now Marylyn, had never borne)
    with just a harmless fiction, though
something Clayfeld did not intend to talk about
    must have occurred. My hunch
is that daft Clayfeld dallied with Ms. Minters,
    that it was her hapless fate
to fall for him, confiding that he try
    the hotel's "luckiest" machine,
for each night after that he landed on
    the triple-cherry combination,

and he came home richer than before he left.
    But soon he drooped again; without
Ms. Minters there, depression seeped into his dream:
    he stood before the one-armed bandit
in his baseball cap, but when the hidden wheel
    clicked out the sentence of his sleep,
black space appeared, and when he shook the mute machine
    to knock an orange into sight,
Clayfeld awoke crack-lipped in the blank mist of dawn.
    One April day, Clayfeld decided
he would visit Grandpa on the farm,
    and, stopping at the local nursery,
he bought twelve three-year-old sweet cherry trees
    to plant upon the hill
with phoebes whistling at him as they once did
    when he summered there.
"Your Grandma tells me that she's going to have
    a baby," Grandpa sighed at dinner,
doffing his worn farm hat to the evening air—
    as if the silent universe
were listening; "it's one chance in a million,
    but if Abraham could do it,
so can I." "Ridiculous! She must be
    almost eighty!" Clayfeld cried.
"It seems to me," I reprimanded Clayfeld,
    "Grandpa pulled your leg. His tease
meant that he's fortunate you still remember him,
    and that you found a chance
to plant another row of cherry trees."

/ Clayfeld Holds On

Shivered by his dream of her into
    a stinging sweat,
Clayfeld awakes in the weatherless dawn
    to find his right hand
has gone numb. As if examining
    a starfish on the beach,
he steadies it, then pokes it with
    a puzzled finger
for some dull, residual response, assumes
    that he has slept on it,
that soon sensation will return, and so
    decides not to disturb
the mood of its glum privacy.
    The same repeating scene,
when first she told him she would leave,
    assembles in his mind:
the cove of swishing lily pads where they
    had landed their canoe,
spied on by golden eyes of bullfrogs startled
    in their grunting
mimickings; the birch tree leaning
    from the slimy bank;
the water snake, uncoiling from its crevice
    in the slop of stones,
sunning along the border of the lake.
    Clayfeld remembers
exactly how the light reflected
    sleek upon the lily pads,
or shadowed inward on the moss
    upon the rocks, or mottled
on the birch tree's blighted leaves,
    but can't bring back
how he had felt—as if he had become only
    the outward story of his life.

He wonders—had he sensed within the gap
    of losing her
some unacknowledged rising of relief
    lifting his thoughts
outside himself into an air so easy
    in the lightness of its flow,
and so impersonal, that nothing moved in him
    besides the patterns
that his eyes perceived? An absent self—was that
    the silence he would vanish in
if he lost even caring for her loss?
    He presses the moist chill
of his stiff hand against the flush
    that swells his ear—
as if the curl and grip of fingers hardened
    his cold hand into a shell
in which he listens to the echoes call
    from the indifferent sea.
Clayfeld is drawn to let himself
    be washed back
with the tide of foaming sand,
    with horseshoe crabs,
starfish and periwinkle, driftwood
    and anemone, but
something deep inside him won't let go:
    he can't give up his memory
of losing her. He feels her loosened hand
    as it released his own
when she stepped out of the canoe,
    pulling herself away
by clinging to the birch; he hears
    the jay's slurred squawk
as its warped shadow passed across the lake.
    And Clayfeld wonders if

she has a child; and now he tries
    imagining her daughter there,
all grown and beautiful, beneath a tree,
    so he can watch her white hand
beckoning to someone who approaches from the glare
    beyond the lake that Clayfeld
has to shade his widened eyes to see.

/ Clayfeld's Illness

Even before he saw her on the day they met
    he sensed that she was there
under the maple by the lake, though maybe
    he remembers it that way
because no longer can he picture her
    as any given age
or know what she became after she left
    so many shaded years ago.
The room vibrates with its chilled light,
    like March sun on a field
of melting snow, yet Clayfeld doesn't
    have to squint to see;
or if he is awake now in *her* dream,
    how can it matter, since
moist, leafy shadows shifting on her hair,
    her woodland scent, move
in his mind as if she were still there.
    The roses on the table
by his bed repose beyond his reach;
    he sees his outstretched hand,

the wrinkled index finger curled,
    and he is sure
he loves the roses swelling red as much
    as when he tended them
to keep the hungry beetles out.
    Now it seems clear — the way
one hears the wholeness of a melody when
    its last, thinning note recedes;
this is the self of memory, freed
    from its clinging grief:
each loved face lost, and yet each loss without
    the need of mourning's soft relief.
Again he sees her sitting on a rock
    beside the lake, watching
a heron lift up from its driftwood perch,
    released from sleep
by its harsh cry, its bill extended
    like a beam of dark,
its slate-blue body focusing the sky.
    Out of her purse she takes
a ring of lapis lazuli that she herself
    has carved with dots
for sun and moon and planets always
    circling in their spheres;
Clayfeld imagines they are random water drops
    or everybody's scattered tears.
Down at the left some crossing lines
    are scratched, perhaps
to indicate a tree, and glistening
    around the burnished stone
a silver frame contains the scene as if
    it were an island in the sea.
She slips his finger in the ring, and now
    the dots begin to multiply

and whirl about until, as on his mother's cameo,
    they form a tranquil face.
She takes Clayfeld's extended hand and draws him
    to her in a watery embrace.

/ Clayfeld's Analysis

Though skeptical, Clayfeld decided, after all,
    he would consult the female analyst
suggested to him by his childhood friend
    whose wife had left him
for an older man. "She listens well,"
    Arthur assured him.
"Perfect for my needs," concluded Clayfeld
    since he was convinced
that women were the cause of his distress —
    he asked too much of them.
As Clayfeld entered Dr. Lovejoy's office,
    he surprised himself, encumbered
by the random surge of blood in an erection;
    quickly Clayfeld crossed his legs
as he sat down in the concealing chair.
    An owl, carved out of stone,
with amber bits for eyes, regarded him
    from Dr. Lovejoy's desk,
and, as if hypnotized, Clayfeld recounted
    his recurrent dreams of falling
in the sea, waving his baseball cap.
    She seemed amused, and Clayfeld sensed
that he had seen her face before. Something about
    her straight lip-line, her gentle eyes,

her oblong ears against her whitened hair,
    convinced him they had met.
Forgetting his old raincoat on the chair,
    Clayfeld walked out puzzled
into the drizzling dusk. And then it came to him:
    Dr. Lovejoy's features,
down to the last, incredible detail,
    were those of Sigmund Freud!
When Clayfeld met Arthur to tell him how
    the hour had gone, his friend gasped,
"I compete with my wife's father's ghost."
    Clayfeld broke in: "The stone owl
seemed to waft an odor of decay, but sweet,
    like fallen, pulpy logs,
steaming in mist after a thunderstorm."
    "All she can talk about,"
his friend replied, "is how her menopause
    has changed her sense of who she is,
and how, with her kids grown, she needs someone to care
    for *her*." Clayfeld's next session brought on
no erection, but a minor nosebleed; he was free
    to gesture with his baseball cap —
although, when Clayfeld noticed that the owl's position
    on the desk had changed, he cringed
because the sculpted bird reminded him
    an owl had raised her young
one summer in the hayloft of their barn.
    He still could picture her
perched on a mat of packed-down crap composed
    of mouse-bone filigree,
and then he realized that Lovejoy's eyes
    were amber like the owl's,
staring at him as if *he* were a field mouse,
    startled in the August grass.

"But Dr. Lovejoy's owl looks like *my* wife,"
    insisted Clayfeld's friend
when they next met, "with hair tufts on her ears,
    her blunt nose, and her twisted face,
alerted just as if an older man
    were coming in the door."
And Clayfeld wondered if Arthur's wife did
    resemble the stone owl,
so when appointment day returned, he scanned
    the amber gaze that seemed
to blink at him; but once again the face
    of Freud appeared: "We must
replace neurotic misery," the master said,
    "with ordinary suffering."
"That's all our cure can hope for," added Lovejoy,
    shaking Clayfeld's hand, but when
he visited his friend, Clayfeld reported that
    a barn owl used to nest
in his back loft. "For weeks I watched her
    tend her young, and I could get
as close as we are now. With wings half-spread,
    and feet set wide apart,
she made a clicking sound like snapping twigs,
    and then, her brown eyes fixed on me,
she slowly rubbed each talon with her chin.
    She fed her babies constantly
with snips of mouse flesh, beak to beak, yet of the eight,
    by summer's end, just four were left.
The strong ones seized the food; I saw the smallest
    eaten by its sister owls."
"That's what owls do," said Clayfeld's friend,
    "but I can't let myself avenge
my mother's death against my wife." Clayfeld
    had never heard his dread

expressed that way before. "I only meant I'm sorry
     your wife left you," Clayfeld said.

/ Clayfeld's Twin

"My dear, indulgent, older (by five minutes) brother,"
     Clayfeld's brother wrote,
"despite your psychic warnings, I have had
     another accident—
my perverse way (no doubt you'll think) of wooing
     Mother Nature's preference:
attention-getting is the cruder way
     of putting it, I know.
So be it, then, here are the gruesome facts:
     I caught a fly-hook
(Parmachene Belle, your favorite) in my left eye
     while fishing with (how's this
for a surprise?) Eileen, my neighbor's wife.
     The doctor still has hope,
but I may lose my sight. There's no help you
     can give right now, so save yourself
time and expense; don't bother coming out.
     Her husband stopped by
at the hospital to say a righteous God
     had punished me. 'An eye
for an Eileen,' quoth I, but, break O heart!,
     the bastard missed my pun."
The smudgy letter blurring as he stared,
     Clayfeld almost could hear
his brother's laughter leaping the abyss
     between them—laughter, he imagined,

that, had Cain possessed it, might have stopped the blow
    that's cursed our whole inheritance.
And yet, a mutilated eye, how could his brother
    laugh that fact away?
Or maybe he was showing off, one more
    bravura boast to demonstrate
he could defy whatever fortune dumped on him,
    as if, although a physicist,
he still required a smirking faith to see
    the quarky universe
of stellar fire-burst or black-hole collapse
    as cosmic comedy.
Clayfeld recalled the day that Bill,
    his sympathetic stepfather,
had his left hand ripped clean off by the combine
    he had worked for years. Could that
have been the origin of Clayfeld's brother's
    proneness to dumb accidents,
the cause, as well, of his disdain for chance?
    Clayfeld remembered Bill just sat there
in the kitchen, stroking Buff's matted fur, his stump
    wrapped in his shirt, waiting
for the ambulance to come. "The kitchen
    needs another coat of paint,"
he joshed, and once again his brother's laugh
    squawked out so coarsely
Clayfeld thought he'd heard the panicked quacking
    of his pet duck, Ishmael,
as if he watched the lunging red fox catch him
    lolling on the muddy shore.
Despite his brother's strictures not to come,
    Clayfeld flew to Los Angeles
to be with him, guessing his stubborn brother
    was too proud to ask,

and yet resenting him for never saying
    bluntly what he felt:
"I'm hurt. I'm scared. I need your help!" Why couldn't
    his own brother simply let
those seething, vexed emotions out?
    "Here lies your blinded, *pun*-
ished, *pupil* of romance, and *cornea* than ever,"
    Clayfeld's brother greeted him.
Shocked Clayfeld had no quip to answer back;
    he pressed his cheek against
the good side of his brother's face and wept—
    sobs surged up from his ribs;
he gagged for breath; a salt stream swamped his lips,
    bubbling with mumbled sounds
of garbled words. "He'll be all right. Don't worry,"
    said the young nurse, holding
Clayfeld's shoulders as he shook; "the bandages
    come off tomorrow and you'll see!"
But Clayfeld's weeping was not finished yet.
    Even his twin did not know
he still harbored all those ancient, unshed tears;
    the sobs kept coming on,
contorting him. Why should his brother's laughter
    be the cause? Clayfeld's gasps
lengthened out to lesser heaves; his moaning
    steadied into measured breaths;
for just an instant, like a baby, he dozed off
    upon his brother's chest. It's true
the nurse thought she heard Clayfeld call for someone—
    "Ishmael?" she asked.
"Is that your brother's childhood name for you?"

/ Sculpting in Stone

Thunder of ripping ice echoes
across the locked river as an ice flow frees itself,
    grinds toward the sea.
Clayfeld observes this absent scene
    as his mind wanders
from the task at hand: sculpting himself
    from the white marble block
he saved for this renewed attempt.
    How shall he tilt the head?
Shall he release the moon-curve of an ear
    toward the window-light
where traffic sounds merge, steady
    as the great, gray breakers
at the first house he remembers by the shore?
    The nose, maybe
he should begin by carving out the nose —
    its twin circles
establishing the body's theme — sniffing
    its blind way out
the marble cave to learn what dangers
    may be here; and then he'd carve
the cheekbone mounds, and the eye sockets
    rounded by the brows,
the egglike eyes with their black nuclei,
    and the O of the lips,
shaped to invent the first word of a cry.
    How close a likeness
to himself should he let mar the symmetry —
    perhaps some little crease
upon the forehead slope to indicate
    the comet of a scar
his brother gave him when he poked him
    with a pointed stick

as they were dueling in the dragon's grove;
  or else the twisted cleft
that wanders to the left side of the chin,
  sinks in, and marks him
as his father's son? Where should the face look—
  eyes fixed straight ahead,
or to the side as if his mother still
  were calling him?
Should he be sitting on a rotted hemlock stump,
  attending to the slow, green
silence of the moss, his hands
  commanded to his knees
as if they might leap up and disobey?
  Or should he shape himself now
striding through the garden to his lover's door—
  the muscles of the thigh
that for this instant bear his weight,
  articulated ridge
by ridge as in a distant mountain range—
  certain she will be waiting
whenever he arrives? Clayfeld cannot decide.
  Again he lets his thoughts
meander where they will; he thinks he hears
  the screaming hiss of ice—
as if a shuddering, new continent
  tears from the arctic pole
to start another geologic age.
  He pictures California
underneath the sea, observing, moon-rapt,
  as the tidal heaves
flood over Arizona, Oklahoma,
  toward the Mississippi
and St. Louis's silver arch, wondering

if the awaited bomb
would have the same effect — as if it, too,
  might be an act of God,
angered as when He parted the Red Sea,
  or just revising
His creation, still somehow delighted
  with inexorable change.
And Clayfeld laughs aloud to realize
  that having watched himself
washed back into the waves, he has survived
  again; he tells the stone,
"*You can't imagine your own death without
  your being someone else,*"
and starts to chip and smooth the marble,
  seeking there inside its space
a circle like the sun, a sphere where anyone
  can find his chosen face.

/ *Clayfeld's Vision of the Next Beginning*

  Neither angels nor devils,
faintly discernible by late starlight,
  spirits adventure overhead
perhaps for pleasure of galactic flight.
  Near the still lake at dawn,
Clayfeld can tell by windless stirring
  in the willow tree
the spirits do look down at us as if
  an instant's glance
is all they need to know our human story
  cooling to its end.

Mountains and cities, forests, gardens, zoos,
    the hives of bees,
plankton dividing daily in the luminous
    decaying seas — everything
is familiar to them. Only our voices
    make them pause: they hear
the laughter in our words detach itself
    from every sorrow
we are born to name — as if our words
    thrive by defying
the one life we have. How can this be?
    wonders solitary Clayfeld
at the spirits' wondering; laughter
    violates the law
that matter must contain itself; the wind
    says always what it says;
water repeats its water sounds upon the stones;
    the prancing bobwhite whistles
its three syllables, then mates forthwith;
    the wolves howl at the border
of their hunting grounds still what they are.
    For each there is
no holding back — the vent of their same sound
    reveals them note by note.
Only our sentences, part snarl, part mating call,
    part longing to restore
the stillness of the past, express us most
    when most we set ourselves
against the body given us to live
    our unevolving death.
But now Clayfeld can see the spirits
    circle back, compelled
by something they have never felt before,
    to mimic us, tempted

by human laughter to breathe themselves
      anew from nothing
that they were. And now they hurtle
      on their way again,
music of speed upon their humming wings.
      Clayfeld can hear our gift
of laughter scatter into seeds of cosmic dust,
      then shudder in the rib
of some limp creature still evolving in his sleep,
      who wakes at windy dawn
beside a lake, beneath a willow tree,
      to find *her* evening name at once
upon his lips. They cleave together now
      in their long passage down the light,
and, pausing to invent the constellations
      of the stars, they bless their unborn heirs
with trilling laughter lifting through the night.

/ Clayfeld the Swimmer

Between Acts I and II of *Turandot*, Clayfeld
      struck up a conversation with
a girl dressed all in shades of blue, and when
      the second intermission came,
to his surprise, Marina asked if he would like
      to drive her to her father's
summer house at Sunrise Lake in northern Maine.
      Her sisters greeted them
(their father had been called away), and after dinner
      each one played an aria for him

until the oldest sister ordered them to bed.
    Clayfeld awoke at dawn,
as usual, and wandered down a pathway
    through the hemlock woods over
a swampy gully dense with spotted touch-me-nots,
    their orange seedpods popping
as he brushed by them; then suddenly
    he thrust out on a rocky shore.
When Clayfeld saw how smooth the water was,
    he stripped down to his underwear
and cartwheeled in. He'd made a ritual that year
    of swimming across lakes
as if that meant he'd claimed them as his own—
    but mainly Clayfeld loved
his body's buoyant flow, the open feeling,
    once he got his stroke in stride,
that he could glide like this forever with his
    rhythmic torso rocking
as his elbow arced above his turning head,
    sweet breath sucked deep
into his lungs, the water-beads cascading
    from his reaching arm that framed
the sun refracted by each water drop.
    Clayfeld would never tire—nothing
could change his gliding in this place, stroke
    after stroke in this splashed light
releasing the approaching colors of the sun.
    But then a sharp pain surged
through Clayfeld's hand—he'd hit his middle finger
    on a floating wooden box. Its lid,
inlaid with one brass square inside a silver square
    inside a gold, was sealed, so Clayfeld
stuck the box into his underwear, and headed back
    where he could get a tool

to pry the box apart. Three eager sisters
    waited for him on the shore, and when,
dry at the house, he forced the lid to open—
    there, rolled neatly like
a miniature scroll, the parchment read:
    What always changes yet remains the same;
    Between extremes retains its lilting name;
    Coming to go in women as in men,
    By emptying refills itself again?
    You only have one life alone to lose,
    So answer this and marry whom you choose.
"My *Soul* reflects the changes of my life,"
    intoned the older sister,
"yet, whatever happens, I remain myself."
    "By giving to another, *Love*
replenishes its source," her sister's voice chimed in.
    "*Water*—" Marina sang out
louder still, "water fits perfectly!
    Whatever vessel holds it
is the shape it takes, and since I guessed the answer,
    Clayfeld, you must marry *me*."
But sleepless in his bed that night, he lay
    suspecting that Marina or
her father had concealed the riddle in the box.
    Uncertain, Clayfeld rose and walked
through ferny dark to hear the echoed notes of stones
    clack on the shore, then he plunged in,
and shivered as his body's weightless glide
    along the rippled water
flowed out smooth and easeful in the moonlit tide.

/ Replacing the Elegy

"The mountain air turns cool
so fast," Marina says to Clayfeld as the last
   opaque red streak of cloud
rubs purple-gray and settles softly in
   the stone-rimmed goldfish pool.
On the repeating slope of stubble fields,
   the corded hay spills down thick shade;
from underneath the eaves the jagged bats
   leap out like blind October leaves
clutching the wind, and through his sleep, an oriole's
   late, liquid nesting call
now loosely trails off incomplete.
   She tells him that before
her mother drowned herself, her mother said,
   "Stay right here on this rock
until your father comes!" As dawn light
   brightened through the mist,
she saw her mother waving from the lake.
   "It seemed so natural,"
Marina says; "I didn't even think to cry.
   The water looked so white.
My father's voice was gentle when
   I woke him up that night."
She leaves the porch to fetch her shawl,
   a moist gleam in her eyes.
Her rocking chair leans after her, swings back,
   begins an agitated creaking,
easing imperceptibly. Clayfeld cannot
   be sure when it goes still;
he hears an echo of her absence rising
   in the blur above the hill.
A goldfish pops the surface of the pool
   which smooths out silver-black,

replacing its familiar daylong images
    of beech and maple leaves.
Hushed Clayfeld shuts his eyes, trying to fix
    the goldfish in his mind—
an instant sunset spilling upside-down,
    a sunrise in the underworld
where everything reverses and refills:
    he sees her mother
swim back in the mist; he sees the baled hay
    suck its shadows in;
a spattering of crows arrives above the hill;
    their caws merge with
the creaking of her chair; her wool shawl
    weaves itself around her arms;
he opens his bestowing eyes—and she is there.
    Clayfeld imagines that
her mother heard the murmuring of waves,
    like wordless lips,
as if *her* mother's voice still summoned her,
    and he can picture
the believing daughter waiting where
    that lichened rock gripped sand,
with early sunlight whitening her hair.
    "We have to go home now,"
her shaking father must have said.
    He reached for his wife's face,
dissolving in the dark, as he bent down that night
    to soothe his daughter into bed.
And now Clayfeld can hear Marina's father ask
    at breakfast in the hazy light,
"Do you want raisins, peaches, blueberries?"
    Among the windless leaves,
still out of sight, an oriole begins to sing,
    and she tells Clayfeld, "Yes,"

that she remembers she replied, "I'd like
    a little bowl of everything."

/ Clayfeld to His Narrator

    Yes, authorizing father, yes,
I know my story's got to entertain;
    you *must* contrive to plot
for me those humbling sorrows, seeking love
    through sexual release, that test
my balled-up character—in phrases measured
    and mellifluously blue
to lull our listeners with song, but spare
    me, please, ordeals of lost love
I lack laughter to endure. Let me still care.
    Don't let my screw-ups turn,
defiant, to a snarl; open my mindful heart
    to love astoundingly beyond
my grasping self; bless me with fruitful days;
    let me beget a son to leave
my blessing to; let my art's fork-tongued praise
    redouble wondering:
a birch grove mirrored undulating in a lake,
    an owl plumped up beneath
the orange circle of a harvest moon,
    its ear-tufts pointed in the breeze
like tips, receding in the lunar haze,
    of misted hemlock trees.
From time to dwindling time, allow me pause
    to watch the purple irises

lean westward from the garden to the sun,
    as if a memory of warmth
rose from their gripping roots and through their stems
    to greet the reddened light,
and held them there until their petals brightened
    to a liquid glow, row upon
waving purple row of pulsing radiance,
    so that a daft observer
like myself could not forget their petals, too,
    turned darker purple, cooling
in their border of piled stones, and darker yet
    with nightfall into redless blue.
Bless me with quietness, I pray, so I can follow
    to an unbegrudging end where
I'm released like lingering last notes
    the meadowlark lets drift away
to join the stillness of the woven air.
    O, grave conceiver of the laughter
of my life, survive, and bless me, not my father
    only but my son as well,
remembering what is to come I hope I will
    have patient love enough to give:
the naming of blue wildflowers in the woods
    as we walk past the waterfall
while searching for the wounded fox's den,
    the body's blind resolve to live.
Remember me with still more blue for longing,
    blue for letting go, forgiveness blue,
the bleak heart's ancient ache for summer things,
    each cherished one a flower
shuddering its name: hepatica and aster,
    larkspur, periwinkle, Jacob's ladder,
gentian, blue-eyed Mary, phlox, and, O!

blue morning glory blossoming
blue-violet, blue-lavender, blue indigo—
    from me, my son, all sung to you,
the breeding woods, the brooding lake, the whole horizon
    flowing bountiful with blue.
Before my fabled life is packed away
    back into breathless dust
and muted clay, let me revive—as if I were
    the laughing, two-faced author
of your epitaph of me—this scene, engraved
    of men composed in harmony,
to bring our empathetic readers true relief,
    not more erected monuments
depicting how love scores its operatic grief:
    a grandfather etched young now
just as he once was; his grandson grown to manhood;
    look! I am there, too, with my
attendant owl carved on its dawn-lit bough.
    Upon the wooden bridge, fishing
the generating lily pond, each line in place, the three
    of us, identical in silhouette,
still as the windless water, sit immutable
    in bluest lapis lazuli.

/ *Clayfeld's Recipe*

To stimulate his dreaming mind before
    he fell asleep, Clayfeld
would sometimes try to reconstruct
    his earliest affairs

that most consumed his heart, recalling
    details such as panties, shoes,
or where they were when they entwined themselves.
    He found it helped to hum
the unresolved chromatic theme from Wagner's
    Tristan und Isolde
or the champagne aria Don Giovanni
    bubbles out when his
unbounded love for womankind
    achieves its burning height.
Then for a change one night, Clayfeld decided
    to experiment and see how much
he could recall about the meals he ate
    those hircine, melancholy days
of his prodigious amorous performances,
    nursing his grievances way back
to Mima his first high-school paramour.
    To his astonishment,
Clayfeld discovered every memory
    his palate could evoke
included some variety of chicken soup —
    as if its piquant tang
still lingered on his tongue. Could something
    about chicken soup, some
combination of ingredients, have the effect
    of a real aphrodisiac?
Clayfeld's research turned up an endless list
    of substances that served once
to arouse the luxury of appetite,
    and most much more fantastic
than our ordinary chicken soup —
    such as a paste concocted
of asparagus, guduchi plants,
    pepper, and licorice,

all boiled in honey, milk, and ghee, which worked,
      according to the *Kama Sutra*,
only in spring. And yet the closest philter
      Clayfeld's careful scholarship
could find to chicken soup was just
      a passing reference
to the blood or excrement of hens,
      though it seemed irrefutable
the form love potions mainly took in every
      place or period—was soup.
Maybe because the soup's aroma—Clayfeld,
      the antiquarian, surmised—
like a burnt offering, could reach the eager
      nostrils of the gods
so that they willingly conferred a portion
      of their procreative power
on our mere, earthbound, bodily desires.
      And speculating thus,
Clayfeld bolts up in bed. He doesn't wish
      to sleep or dream; he only
wishes for the slick of simmered chicken soup
      upon his lips and tongue;
he wants the warm flow soothing down his throat
      to his cramped, childless groin;
he wants the tangy hint of marrow bones,
      soft carrots sweetening,
thickened with celery and onions, sharpened
      with ground peppercorns
and several pinches of rough sea salt—
      a holy harvest of true
flavored harmony, the consummation that
      the yearning mortal mouth
may most devoutly wish! Clayfeld indeed has known
      the nectar of the gods;

just sitting there in bed, in hand a cup
    of chicken soup with rice,
Clayfeld at last declares out loud in love
    that he has entered paradise.

/ *Clayfeld's Metamorphosis*

Despite his nightly cup of chicken soup,
    Clayfeld once more was looking
greenish-wan, his underlying melancholy
    showing puffy through his skin;
his panting speech had slowed and deepened
    to a raspy grumble
rising like a spasm, so it seemed to him, up
    from his belly and his lungs.
Out to the lake at dawn to swim, slave
    to his summertime routine,
went hopping Clayfeld over dale and field,
    ravine and rivulet —
alive, yes, puzzled glad his body was,
    despite himself, to be alive!
Pale, swirling mist, like flower petals floating
    in the thickened air, converged
and gathered into fleshly shape through some trick
    of the fertilizing wind,
and moved toward him, and made a little hollow,
    like a scallop shell, where water ruffled,
turning in its filigree of foam, and sighed upon
    the flotsam on the shore.

"O! O! O! O!" she said, her round, white arms
    across her breasts, her wheat-gold hair
unbound, awry, "I didn't think I'd find you here."
    And Oh!, and Clayfeld
with an Ah! that panged him to his ribs
    knew surely he had witnessed
Venus rising from the sea. Her name was Evelyn,
    and, no, she'd never seen
the Botticelli painting Clayfeld babbled on about
    as if "The Birth of Venus"
could explain why they had met. Quite simply,
    Evelyn had grown up by the lake;
she, also, liked to start her day with a long swim,
    although this was the first time
that she'd ventured to swim all the way across
    to Clayfeld's side. And Clayfeld's
pent-up sorrow heedlessly leapt pouring forth:
    he needed to be loved for laughter
unreleased in him; if someone only recognized
    inherent joy lived there—
he clasped his chest—then he would be transformed
    the way despondent Mozart plucked
pure music from potentiality of air.
    "I've got to go—I won't forget—
I promise that I won't forget!" and Evelyn
    plunged back into the lake as if
possessive Neptune summoned her away,
    while Clayfeld, desolate,
lay back exhausted on the beach to brood.
    Not having heard from Evelyn
a drizzling week, Clayfeld turned greener still;
    his voice croaked even more;
and then, one cloudless morning with cooled Clayfeld
    freshly dripping from his swim,

a blue, beribboned, cardboard carton,
    three by six, arrived by
Mercury Express—from Evelyn. His heart
    athump, he opened it
with sticky hands: black, staring, bulbous eyes,
    a gold crown tilted on its head,
its arms akimbo, squatting there serene—a frog,
    stitched up the size of a grown man,
winked straight at him and, leaning forward,
    boomed out, "GROO!" as if
to woo the back row of an opera house.
    Clayfeld took two jumps back,
but then regained his poise; with Evelyn's
    low O calls echoing
across the lake, he snatched the frog's crown
    from his head and placed it on his own.
Believing surely she would be the one
    who'd wake old laughter buried
in his heart, bold Clayfeld, like a prince, stretched out
    to strut forth human in the sun.

/ Clayfeld Proposes For Good

"Since people are the means
by which computers reproduce themselves," Clayfeld
    hypothesized before his mirror,
razor blade in hand, "it follows logically
    future Darwinians
will think of us as gabbing genitals—
    unless we humans learn

to re-create ourselves anew from our own words.
    I won't allow myself to fall
in love impassively," Clayfeld spieled on,
    "as if my mother's image
programmed me like an imprinted duck. Rather,
    to rise in love by giving
flesh to words, like music to the wanting air,
    in acting out a vow — that's how
I'll free myself from servitude to women
    I have hopelessly adored
whose hormones were not tuned to hear my pleas!"
    And thus determined, Clayfeld nicked
the animal that lurked beneath his skin;
    although he winced and bled,
he felt that his decision had been made: he would
    propose to Evelyn despite
his qualms about her motives for desiring *him*.
    And yet, he thought, one final test
of Evelyn's commitment would be wise.
    Clayfeld was certain that of all
the differences between the sexes culture
    had imposed — and therefore could reverse —
one vast abyss, set in our genes, no doubt,
    when primal ooze first trembled
at a thunder crash, remained unbridgeable:
    women do not like music played
as loudly as most men insist it should be played.
    And so Clayfeld devised his test:
if Evelyn got angry, she was not for him,
    but if she laughed — in spirit
thus negating the negation of the limits
    nature binds us in — he'd pledge himself
to her for one full, marital eternity.
    That night, before they started

making love, contriving Clayfeld programmed
 his expensive stereo to play
the great climactic scene where the Commandant's
 vengeful marble statue comes
to interrupt Don Giovanni's gormandizing,
 setting the volume dial higher
than its usual position for the fiery fray.
 As all their passions mounted,
heated Clayfeld raised the volume when the statue
 clasps Don Giovanni's hand
and offers him a last chance to repent.
 "Together! Now!" cried Clayfeld,
louder than the orchestra's D-minor din,
 just as the Don screams "No!"
and "No!" again, again, again. But later,
 in the eased G-major aftermath,
sly Evelyn sighed, "Darling, I'm afraid
 you lost me on the final 'No!'"
"I'll put the sextet on once more," responded
 Clayfeld quickly, "if you'll marry
me, peasant Masetto, now that the Don is dead—
 'Questo è il fin di chi fà mal!'"
he choired according to the harmony resolved
 in his deliberated heart,
as if, now bound for good, he'd found in Mozart's
 mirthful ending, his true part.

/ Clayfeld Renews His Vow to Evelyn

Weeding the garden, Clayfeld sprained his finger
    pulling out a stubborn root,
and had his ring cut off—the wedding ring
    Evelyn's mother had passed on
to Evelyn which she in turn bestowed on him—
    because his finger swelled so much.
For safekeeping, he sealed it in an envelope
    and filed it with his tax receipts,
planning to have the heirloom welded whole again
    as soon as his offending
eggplant-purple finger shrank to size.
    When Clayfeld looked for it
after an interval of one full year,
    the ring had disappeared;
Clayfeld suspected Evelyn had hidden it
    to dramatize her point:
he carelessly neglected his accounts.
    Clayfeld refused, however,
to admit to her that he had lost the ring,
    hoping somehow it would turn up,
or he'd discover where she'd hidden it.
    One clear May morning Clayfeld
went out hiking in the budding woods
    to hunt the most delectable
of mushrooms, true morels, which one can find,
    if lucky, underneath an oak,
their heads protruding from decaying leaves
    on pallid stems. But not that day.
"We'll do without morels this year," grumped
    Clayfeld to his mushroom pouch.
Spying an unfamiliar butterfly upon
    a rotting hemlock stump,
Clayfeld stalked closer, and, incredibly, a ring
    gleamed through a spider's web

amid the dew, so like his own, he wondered
  if his wife had put it there —
a likely place his mushroom hunt would lead him to.
  Clayfeld attempted to recall
the pattern etched so clearly on his ring:
  crossed lines suggesting birds
above an undulating stream. He counted twelve;
  that's more, he thought, than he remembered —
yet, how many rings could have designs like that?
  He slid it on as if it were
his own lost ring, deciding he would bluff:
  he'd try insisting to his wife
he'd had the ring repaired two months ago.
  And then, inspired by his abiding
father's ghost, Clayfeld conceived his coup de grâce,
  although at dinner he
betrayed surprise when smiling Evelyn
  served him morels sautéed
in pepper butter, delicately sliced.
  But she responded with:
"Don't worry — these morels, my dear, were picked
  in our own friendly woods;
I wouldn't unintentionally poison you!"
  Prepared, Clayfeld pretended
so convincingly, he almost could believe
  that, tasting, he had started
to hallucinate, chanting incantatory
  vatic cadences: "I see my soul,
its debt redeemed, a golden butterfly, transfigured
  from the fallen dross of earth,
now rising toward the sun, its final home!"
  "O, Clayfeld," Evelyn implored,
"please don't abandon me to this dull vale of tears!"

"I won't," Clayfeld replied, "if you'll
take me to be your awe-full husband once again.
    Inside this box I have a ring
engraved with triangles resembling darting fish;
    I had forgotten that my father
left it to me in his will." While kissing her,
    he placed it on the finger
of his twice betrothéd Evelyn, and relished —
    like a hummingbird that sips
sweet nectar from a rose — the taste of "Yes, I do,"
    still lingering upon her lips.

/ Clayfeld's Infancy

Clayfeld was working on a bust of Freud,
    depicting how he looked
midway in an analysis before
    cancer stiffened his jaw,
aware he found his female patients still
    provocative. Almost concealed
between the moustache and the beard, Freud's lip-line
    tilted upward to the left
too radically, in baffling contrast
    with the glum droop on the right.
Clayfeld had not intended to portray
    a failed truce in his face,
and yet he could not coax the stone to some
    more peaceful symmetry.
"I'll leave it, jarring as it is," and Clayfeld
    stalked out in the bare, November wind

to calm himself by walking through the pine woods
  to the lake. Above the ridge,
just where the lake in autumn becomes visible,
  a fox's skeleton
reposed among the matted leaves, its head
  not yet completely decomposed—
although the rib cage, perfectly intact,
  glowed in the hazy light.
A swirl of wind wound past the upper pines,
  descended, gasping in the leaves,
then murmured through the rib cage of the fox—
  a hollow note, earth's old
Aeolian refrain of wind upon a bone.
  And Clayfeld's memory spun back
to when his father had to amputate
  the oozing toes that dangled
from the baby fox he rescued from the trap,
  its glossy eyes staring,
not at his father, but at him. He nursed the fox
  all summer long, but couldn't tame it,
so he let it go; and late that wintry March,
  at mating time, he saw it leap
across the brook into the sloping field,
  its tail outstretched, and then
limp silently over the settled snow.
  For the first time, incredibly,
another memory came whirling back:
  Clayfeld must have been two years old—
it was his parents' anniversary;
  his father wrapped a red fox stole,
with staring heads, around his mother's neck;
  he kissed her from behind,
his rough beard merging with the fox's fur.
  As dumbstruck Clayfeld stood

transfixed, still gazing at the skeleton,
    the shining harp of ribs
again wailed in the wind, melodious.
    What happened next, no doubt,
was Clayfeld's reconstruction from a story
    that his mother must
have told to him: some time before his birth—
    because Clayfeld had started
thrashing in the womb, pressing his head
    against her throbbing artery
to feel her pulse—his mother thought music
    might relax him, so she went to hear
the Philharmonia play Mozart, and, by God,
    it worked! After that concert,
Clayfeld seemed to float around at ease, secure
    in that he would enjoy
what was awaiting him. But Clayfeld, to this day,
    insists he actually
remembers hearing Mozart in the womb.
    "If apple trees produce
their fullest fruit when Mozart's symphonies
    are played for them—there's proof
of that," he said, "why can't a fetus
    sweeten to such music too?"
One has to grant Clayfeld his point, although,
    returning from the skeleton,
he left his twisted face of Freud unchanged
    inside his windless studio.

/ *Clayfeld Is Summoned*

By special messenger at dawn,
a telegram arrives at Clayfeld's door
    summoning him to court
that very morning at exactly 9:03.
    "What have I done?" Clayfeld
cries out, his palms clapped to his shallow ears,
    his head thrown back as if
the moon above his chimney smoke were listening,
    although the messenger
has vanished down the road among the pigeons
    scattering the pebbled dust.
"And whom have I run over recently?"
    defiant Clayfeld dryly
challenges the hollow air, then feels chagrined.
    "This could be serious,"
he reprimands himself. When Clayfeld sees
    that his red Skylark's
right front tire is flat, he hastily
    puts on the sagging spare,
but the malevolent ignition whines and conks—
    the battery is dead. So Clayfeld
dials a cab, pressing the digits 9-0-3,
    and Lo! a limousine appears,
long like an ambulance, black like a hearse,
    flashing its ice-blue lights,
and there goes Clayfeld speeding into town.
    When the car stops before
the court's processional of stairs,
    the driver, in a cloak
concealing bony shoulder blades, asks Clayfeld
    in an irritated voice,
"Did I deliver you here yesterday?"
    Astonished at how many steps

lead up to the Ionic columns soaring
    on the portico, Clayfeld
beholds the great carved doors swing open
    as a flood of people
crowd upon the marble stairs so tightly
    that he can't ascend.
He waves his golden, thirteenth-birthday fountain pen,
    and instantly the people part
to form a path, dividing like the walled Red Sea,
    so Clayfeld can pass through.
The judge steps out into the sunlit plaza
    from his inner shade,
a pigeon on his shoulder, and a nurse —
    a bandage covering her eyes —
with shapely ankles (Clayfeld can't help but observe)
    holds out a silver scale
that balances an infant on each side.
    "Are they asleep?" inquires
hushed Clayfeld cautiously, "are they alive?"
    "Choose one," the judge decrees,
and may you and your wife be three times blessed."
    His wailing son clutched in his arms,
Clayfeld, father at last, descends the stairs
    to unconstrained applause
from everyone assembled there — until he hears
    their thrumming hands like wings
blur in a distant meadow with the humming
    of innumerable clover bees.
"It's your turn now to feed him," softly
    Clayfeld's wife repeats,
"and I still promise you it won't be long
    before you are rewarded
by a whole night filled with honeyed sleep."

Outside his dusty window
in a sun shower, Clayfeld, now stark awake, can see
three cooing mourning doves
circle the dripping hemlock tree.

/ Clayfeld Prunes His Apple Trees

I might have been a rabbi, Clayfeld thought,
holding the soft tip
of a newly planted apple tree as if
it were a little penis
to be consecrated with a blessing
and a skillful snip.
Just as the Lord made His abiding covenant
with father Abraham and all his seed
by instituting circumcision as a token
of their bond, so, too, would Clayfeld
sanctify his love for what he tended
in the garden of *his* care.
And as God changed old Abram's name
to Abraham, Clayfeld—
still lording it to entertain himself—
picked Pentateuchal names
for his adopted family of trees as he
went snipping down the rows
along his hillside in a tilted flood
of rising southern light.
"Be fruitful, Shem; be fruitful, Ham; Japheth,
beget and multiply!"
Clayfeld commanded with his pruning shears,
pointing at each new tree,

like Adam naming creatures of the field,
    for Adam's name, just like his own,
evoked the very soil from which he came.
    A snip of foreskin
wasn't much, Clayfeld surmised, if it appeased
    a jealously protective God,
though Clayfeld hoped his son, now eight days old,
    would never have to fear
such speechless blame as when his father's stroke
    had locked his tongue,
making his death, at last, unmerciful.
    Distracted, Clayfeld clipped
his left thumb's pulpy end with his dull shears
    and stood there with it
in his mouth as if he could assuage
    whatever pain might come
by savoring the salt taste of his blood.
    A groundhog at the orchard's edge
returned his stare and grimaced, drawing back
    into his hidden hole,
while Clayfeld, furious at his own clumsiness,
    waving his shears, flashed
UP YOURS! at the groundhog's disappearing grin,
    then waited limply, thumb in mouth,
as blunt wind spread his tears about his face,
    hassling the apple trees.
Another wail of wind among the clouds
    above the mountain peaks released
the swirling light to fill a widening expanse
    of the advancing sky—and then,
as if Jehovah heard imploring Abraham
    call out in Clayfeld's voice
for some assuring sign, a double rainbow
    arched across the orchard field.

/ 65

"Not bad for my first miracle!" Clayfeld exclaimed
    to his adoring apple trees,
his shears bestowing benedictions one by one
    until the rainbow faded back
into the ordinary dusk. And Clayfeld
    boasted to his wife that night,
"A rainbow for my apple trees should keep
    my son's respect!" But Evelyn,
exhausted from her minor miracle, was strolling
    through the fragrant grove of sleep.

/ His Mother's Miracle

When Clayfeld gave up smoking years ago,
    he dreamed that he auditioned
for the part of Scarpia in the premiere of *Tosca*.
    "Yours!" declared Puccini,
"but it's my conception that this character—
    the flames of lust consuming him—
smokes constantly throughout Act II." "I can't," protested
    Clayfeld, "please, I made a vow;
my confidence in my own will's at stake."
    "One must make sacrifices
for one's art," intractable Puccini said,
    "so we can bear in song
what otherwise would be unbearable."
    Clayfeld refused, yet when
the doctor called from Arizona, telling him
    his mother had a heart attack,
"Fly out!" Clayfeld slumped in a rear seat of the plane,

pleasure of smoke grating his throat
down to his lungs returning instantly.
    "I doubt she'll hold on
through the night," the doctor muttered. "Let her die
    peacefully in her bed;
don't try to get her to the hospital."
    "I'm still not ready yet,"
his mother pleaded as he sat by her,
    stroking the puffed, blue veins
that gasped along her hands, "not ready yet . . ." And then,
    surprisingly, her voice sped up:
"You'd better have the window washer come, the house
    looks dusty; whether I recover now
or not, it's certain we'll be having visitors."
    Her breathing eased, she slept,
and Clayfeld walked out in the Arizona dusk.
    He smoked and prayed to nothing
he believed as silhouettes of saguaro arms
    reached out as if imploring
some unheeding desert deity for rain.
    Why had he dreamed he sought
the role of Scarpia, that Nazi prototype—
    sadistic hate derived
from thwarted love? Assigning him a human
    motivation even for the sake
of song seemed now to grieving Clayfeld cowardice
    avoiding fact: the fact of power
brutalizing all our species' history.
    Clayfeld feared something in his mind
must have assented to his own, his mother's,
    everybody's death, and now *thought*
twisted him to seek revenge against himself
    for his compact with death.

When Clayfeld woke up thrashing in the morning,
      having dreamed that Tosca stabbed him
as he tried to rape her—Scarpia's dying
      music liquid on his lips—
miraculously, propped against the kitchen sink,
      his mother stood in slippers
sister Ida once had sent from Venice,
      making matzoh balls, moror,
gefilte fish, her secret recipe, for Passover.
      "It's just one week away," she said,
"*dayenu* if you can remain to help me
      celebrate this year."
So Clayfeld stayed. Once more the Lord inflicted
      plagues on the Egyptians;
Clayfeld's ancestors fled free beneath
      the desert sun, surviving
on unleavened bread. But Clayfeld's mother
      had used up her miracle.
She died, alone, before another Seder
      came around, not having kept
her promise next year she'd come east to pray
      in Clayfeld's godless house.
After his mother's funeral, Clayfeld stopped
      smoking one more time, vowing
this was his last. He closed his eyes, determined
      never to forget his mother's
single miracle—she had by will, *dayenu*,
      chosen somehow to survive
beyond the time allotted her, and Clayfeld
      focused on those pictures
he remembered never having steeled himself
      to look at carefully:
he watched thick smoke curl like the necks of horses
      wildly shaking their black manes

across the blowing sunlit winter blue
    above the camps at Buchenwald,
while chanting to himself, *dayenu*, barely
    audible upon his lips,
day-day-enu, dayenu, dayenu.

/ Clayfeld Atones

A foot of snow descended in the night;
    their road was drifted in.
"No need to wake the kids for school," Clayfeld
    decided, swaddled still
in his own stumbling body's drowsy heat.
    A long, relieving pee — as if
a fountain satyr spouted in some Gothic park —
    pleased Clayfeld as he followed
his routine: he strolled into the kitchen,
    watching the steam uncurling
from his friendly coffee mug in genie shapes
    that vanished like his children
climbing with their sleds beyond the ridge
    onto an unfamiliar hill.
Clayfeld was startled from his reverie,
    confounded to observe
his coffee had no taste or smell. Suspiciously,
    he sniffed it harder,
sloshed it on his panicked tongue, but though
    he still could tell that he
had liquid in his mouth, the only real sensation
    Clayfeld could identify

was absence: absence palpably was *there*.
    Although he could enjoy
a sneeze emitted by surprise, deliberate
    blowing of one's nose
disgusted Clayfeld, yet he blasted out
    a shofar note that could have filled
the synagogue at Yom Kippur, to clear
    his sinuses, expecting
such purgation would restore his taste buds
    to their prelapsarian estate.
But when his wailing ram's horn failed, Clayfeld
    was forced to realize he felt
afraid. What made his body punish him?
    Had he not fed and fondled it,
praising its skills, as if he showed a mother's pride
    in a precocious child?
Or had he doted on his body to excess?
    Vexed Clayfeld pressed his gums to see
if once again his teeth were loosening,
    and he blasphemed the air
with an accusatory fist: "O taste buds,
    why have you forsaken me?"
Tears filled a crease by Clayfeld's mouth—
    but then, to his delight,
he tasted them, sloshing his resurrected tongue
    along his lips to prove
indeed a trace of salt abided there.
    Reprieved, he laced his boots,
tightened his furry hat about his ears,
    hoisted his son's new sled,
and bellywhopped into the January dawn.
    Three runs were all he needed
to stir up a sweat, so Clayfeld stamped back
    in the house, returned to bed,

wondered if he should make love to his wife,
    but let her sleep since she alone
had tended their sick baby earlier that night.
    He heard the hastened snow
slide swishing from the laden hemlock trees,
    remembering his mother sway
beside her fire, and sank into a deeper doze,
    intoning slowly, underneath
his breath, to keep the dwindling whisper
    of himself from falling still:
rock-a-bye Clayfeld when the wind breaks
    high up on that high hill.

/ Calling for Help

    Clayfeld tried to recall
the morning when that ghostly voice first moaned
    for help, but his hypothesis —
based on the time he fell out of the boat
    when he was four, while fishing
with his father — seemed unable to explain
    why water echoing
inside the shower stall should bring
    hallucinations on: he'd hear
the lost, forsaken voice, and then say to himself,
    "It isn't there," but still
he'd have to shut the shower off in order
    to be absolutely sure.
Clayfeld did not believe in extrasensory
    phenomena, and yet

he could not quite suppress a surge of fear
    that warned him the faint voice
ought to be heeded as a prophecy:
    "Prepare yourself," he thought,
when he had turned the shower back on,
    "someday your son or daughter
may need rescuing." Clayfeld had read
    one psychic claimed he sometimes
tuned in on a stranger's life as if phone wires
    got crossed; likewise, uncannily,
Clayfeld suspected someone out there needed help.
    Clayfeld would dry himself,
but sweat stuck to him afterwards until
    the weird sensation passed away.
Once, Clayfeld heard the voice outside his bathroom door,
    and then his wife was calling him,
although, "I'm leaving, dear," could hardly count
    as anybody's cry for help.
Despite certainty that *no voice was there*,
    Clayfeld still heard a forlorn voice
call to him with increasing frequency,
    and, for relief, he'd turn
the water's temperature as high as human skin
    could tolerate the heat—
as if that cry were *there* inside his flesh
    and might be steamed away.
Clayfeld was finishing a scaled-down statue
    of his fishing son,
his lean, unmuscled boy's arm tightening
    in the completed instant
of the casting of a fly just as the trout
    struck taking in the hook,
when Clayfeld thought he heard the cry again:

the trout, it was the trout!
It was the disbelieving cry of wounded flesh!
    Clayfeld worked on—he needed
to show grace incarnate in the statue's poise:
    he thickened the boy's shoulders,
shaped a little bulge along his calves
    and up his moistened thighs,
retouching every artery and swell
    that shadowed through his skin,
until he realized that he'd transformed the boy
    into a full-grown man.
"So be it," bowing, flourishing his scraper,
    Clayfeld said, leaving his studio
almost at dawn to go to bed. With shoes in hand,
    he tiptoed through their room, careful
not to disturb his wife. "Daddy, is that you?"
    Evelyn called out from the deep past
her sleeping warmth contained, which Clayfeld,
    trembling, edged himself into
as still another watchful voice repeated,
    like an echo, "Is that you?"

/ Clayfeld's Narrator Interrupts

"In the beginning God created every living
    orgasm," were Arthur's parting words
the last time Clayfeld saw his lifelong friend.
    Despite the fact that his first wife
had left him for an older man, Arthur,
    although remarried, still

could not resist the brief, rejuvenating
  charm of an affair.
Now, reader, let me reconstruct: Arthur
  dies of a heart attack
while sleeping with his lover in New York;
  but she can't bring herself to phone
Arthur's still unsuspecting wife, and thus
  at 3:00 a.m. Clayfeld is clanged
from bed, dreading a neutral voice will say:
  "Your son has had an accident."
That's possible—I have such fears, thinks Clayfeld
  in my thoughts, although if this
were my own story, *my* friend's lover never
  would have called to waken me.
In my own untold life, I also worry that my son
  and daughter drive too fast,
but they were home the night *my* lifelong friend expired
  in Boston making love. Clayfeld's wife
urges that he must inform widowed Rebecca
  where Arthur is and how
he passed away, but Clayfeld leaves some details out
  because he wants no one to judge
Arthur's compulsive need to hide his life from death.
  What more forsaken place to hide,
thinks Clayfeld, than inside a pumping body dumbly
  doing what all bodies do, as he
returns to bed, *makes marriage* (Clayfeld's euphemism)
  with his wife, then dozes
in the aftermath—with white Rebecca watching
  in her negligee, the warm phone
moist against her ear. His wife shakes him to stop
  his dream-spilled muttering,
trying to soothe him with: "There's nothing more
  a friend can do; life doesn't end

the consummating way love wants it to."
    Clayfeld imagines Arthur
begging for forgiveness, smiting his breast,
    biting his lips as if
to find flesh for his reconciling words—
    but Clayfeld still remains
uncertain whether he can tell Rebecca something
    at the funeral to comfort her
without betraying what he knows. So after
    eulogizing Arthur's love
for every organism underneath God's sun,
    his appetite for all cuisines—
not just desserts—(yes, Arthur would have liked that pun)
    Clayfeld, fork-tongued, embraced Rebecca,
pressing his flushed cheek upon her baffled tears.
    "What sense is there," she asked,
"if nothing is complete?" "Arthur's last words to me
    were that he loved you," Clayfeld heard
his rehearsed voice intone. Next morning Clayfeld
    drove back home through yellow mist,
his hand on his wife's thigh as if that gesture
    spoke his silent heart for him.
"Please drive with both hands on the wheel," she said,
    then added as an afterthought,
"With Arthur gone, who'll chortle at your puns?"
    Reader, Rebecca, muse
of epitaphs, forgive the words that surged unbidden
    and so singular to Clayfeld's lips
to mourn his unrepentant friend. Clayfeld replied:
    "The night I heard the news
of Arthur's death, I felt relieved it wasn't
    our own son who died."

/ Clayfeld's Campaign

Glum Clayfeld was defeated three to one
    in his attempt to get elected
to the high-school board, having assumed
    that with the help of friends
he might dissuade the stamping local herd
    of vengeful culture-tramplers
not to cut the budget for the glee club
    and the orchestra.
"Next time I'll run for dogcatcher,"
    grouched Clayfeld to his wife
across his scrambled eggs. But then, half-shaved,
    ascending to the toilet seat
as if it were a podium, his arms outstretched,
    Clayfeld proclaimed to all
the grunting voters waiting for his words:
    "Your dignity and mine, take note
my countrymen, requires that I conduct you up
    to harmonies sublime,
and thus, without base airs, I will compose myself
    to scale the heights of office now!"
Applause from Clayfeld's daughter, son, and wife,
    assembled at the bathroom door,
erupts and gathers to a cheering multitude
    of echoes in the shower stall
where earlier Mozart's Sarastro had intoned
    these hallowed halls to be a place
where vengeance is unknown. "Clayfeld for president!"
    conspiring wife and children chanted
with the puzzled howling of old Buff:
    "Our glee club will survive
forevermore in the curriculum!"
    At dinnertime that night, election
strategy was born when Clayfeld told his kids,
    "We need a fighting slogan

on our bumper stickers and our button pins
    that woos all tone-deaf voters
to our cause, for angels speak to mortal ears
    either in laughter or in song."
And thus "MUSICIANS DO IT RIGHT ON TIME" became
    the campaign slogan Clayfeld thought
would sweep him into power and keep harmony
    in Greensville. But, on write-in votes
from his retaliating friends, shocked Clayfeld
    was elected dogcatcher,
and, at the celebration of his victory,
    they gleefully assured him
his belief that *all things suffering have souls*
    prepared him for the job.
So Clayfeld tuned his art to sculpting snoozing dogs,
    like Rembrandt's lion etchings, or,
with Buff his model sniffing upwind for good news,
    Clayfeld depicted happiness
inherent in reposing flesh and bone.
    Immortal Buff, yawning in bronze,
was purchased by the Greensville veterinarian
    to honor empathetic Clayfeld,
since the dog-pound's records showed that
    in his term as dogcatcher
more homes were found for stray, abandoned dogs
    than in the previous decade
before Clayfeld heard civic duty twang
    the unsung discords
of the little power given him to help
    with so much wrong.

/ Clayfeld's Operatic Debut

Clayfeld considered Rita the most gifted student
    he had taught in years
at Greensville University where Clayfeld's
    basic sculpture course
in structure and material was famous
    in the dorms as Bones and Stones.
"You have the touch," Clayfeld assured her
    when her confidence was down
one sleeting afternoon as they were in his studio
    discussing her rough sketches
for a lifesize sculpture of herself.
    Tears came to Rita's eyes;
"I only told him that his student singers
    are inspired by him," she said,
"and then Professor Hornblow propositioned me."
    Fire springing to his cheeks,
Clayfeld cried out, "My God, he's older than I am!"
    Professor Hornblow was contrite
when Clayfeld icily confronted him, pleading
    he would reform if Clayfeld promised
not to file a sexual harassment charge.
    "I've suffered punishment enough,"
he said, "just knowing what I know about myself."
    To his surprise, Clayfeld then swore
he would say nothing to the dean if Hornblow
    offered him the part
of Mephistopheles in *Faust* to be premiered
    at Greensville in the spring.
"I know the role by heart," Clayfeld, amused,
    could hear himself proclaim, and so
the two of them shook hands to seal the compact
    that began their partnership.
Clayfeld's interpretation of the character
    was that, no less than agéd Faust,

desire for lasting youth consumed the Devil's heart;
    desire for more desire
had poisoned Satan's love for endless love
    into its jealous opposite.
Clayfeld on stage would stare past Faust,
    twirling his waxed mustachios,
flashing his *you-must-pay-the-rent* wide grin
    at every woman in his view —
each face, he thought, was beautiful if ever
    he could know her well enough —
but sympathetic longing swelled so thick
    in Clayfeld's throat,
his throbbing voice took on a dark vibrato
    trembling from his bones,
that vindicated Hornblow's bargain giving him
    the chance to sing the part.
"We all contain a world of hidden selves
    demanding birth; the sculptor must
release them into light," Clayfeld espoused
    to Rita much more formally
than he had planned, stiffly hugging her farewell
    that humid graduation day.
"I hope in time you will be proud of what
    I've learned from you," she said,
and vanished with her parents in the crowd.
    "A chauvinist Pygmalion
is what I am," Clayfeld tried to cheer himself,
    but he remained dejected, working
through the summer on a statue of his daughter
    sitting on a rock, her weight
thrown back upon her thin, unsteady arms,
    her face upturned to catch the sun.
"Her features could be anyone's," hissed Clayfeld to himself
    as Hornblow's tenor voice

accompanied his knocking at the door
    of Clayfeld's dusty studio.
"*Me voici!*" Clayfeld mellifluously greeted him
    as usual with mockery.
But fleshier than he remembered her, a shawl
    around her belly and her shoulders
like a hunched owl's wings disturbed for flight,
    Rita appeared at Hornblow's side:
"We wanted you to be the first to know;
    we ask your blessing," Rita said.
Clayfeld could not complete the statue
    of his daughter, though he tried
until October when the flailing trees,
    ablaze, revealed their branches
to the wind, and Clayfeld then decided with relief
    that he, as Mephistopheles,
cast out and wailing on the earth, at best could ease
    his own disfigured mind
by leaving her still struggling to find shape, and bent
    just like the twisted slaves
of Michelangelo, who, pushing out in labor from
    confining stone, needing to laugh
or groan or sing, seem puzzled to be leaving home,
    their first, white, silent element.

/ Clayfeld's Daughter Reveals Her Plans

"A feast of light!" Clayfeld proclaimed
while waiting for his daughter to appear.
    Surveying the horizon

from his own dear hill where he and Evelyn
    had lived for thirty years,
Clayfeld watched sunset-orange stream across the field
    beneath the altocumulus
configuration of ribbed clouds that formed
    a vast, arched passageway
that magnified the light by whirling it
    up from the meadow to the clouds
and back again as if such mirroring
    of brazen orange
burnishing itself would never end.
    The clouds then sealed the sun
behind the mountain top; the buried light was gone
    as if a black hole's pull
had sucked it from the valley: Clayfeld let
    a little gasp escape despite
the many times he'd witnessed this same scene.
    Stunned Clayfeld ruminated
he had never seen a sunset end so fast,
    and that, perhaps, accounted
for the gust of calm despondency — like mist
    unfurling on a morning lake —
that wafted through his mind . . . yes, *calm*, since after
    all these watchful years,
Clayfeld could now take pleasure even
    in his somber autumn moods.
"The whole shebang, from A to Z, one must
    embrace it all!" resounding
Clayfeld sermonized into the sullen dark.
    The clouds had drifted on:
now Capricorn peered down the southern sky
    across the zodiac
as Cynthia arrived, pale and disheveled
    from her long day's drive.

"Mom knows why I've come home to talk to you.
     I'm planning to get married, Dad,
in just one month." "She knows? Your mother knows?"
     astonished Clayfeld blathered
to his daughter at the entryway. "His ancestors
     rebuilt their Maryland estate
after the Civil War, and, like his grandfather,
     he plans to run for Congress."
Sexual congress was the quip that Clayfeld
     managed to suppress.
"I brought a present, Dad," and, for an instant,
     Clayfeld's spirits lightened
as she handed him a box with horses leaping
     neatly over rocky streams.
"And what the hell is this?" demanded Clayfeld's
     disappointed, high-pitched voice.
"A hunting horn, Dad," Cynthia replied.
     "Two days before the wedding
there will be a fox hunt for the special guests,
     and you've been honored
to begin it with the blowing of this horn.
     George Washington loved fox hunting,
and Thomas Jefferson, and . . ." "Fox hunting!"
     flushed Clayfeld bellowed out,
"a fucking fox hunt thought up by some sterile,
     syphilitic, lisping English earl
to titillate himself, and you want me
     parading on their lawn
in Mr. Mincing Blueblood's scarlet britches
     and my yarmulke—
or maybe I should wear my baseball cap?—
     tooting my brains away?"
Clayfeld, disconsolate, stamped from the room

with Evelyn pursuing him:
"For once you've got to trust what Cynthia
    decides is right for her!"
So on the day assigned, proud Clayfeld stood there
    in his baseball cap, intractable,
defiant, as the umber sun rose up
    behind the humid trees
and spread its haze along the whitewashed fences
    crossing through the field
to the ravine that marked the forest's edge.
    Like one of Joshua's priests,
summoned to Jericho, he lifted up his horn
    and wailed the hollow signal
to the straining dogs to let the hunt commence.
    And then, unheard amid the din,
distracted Clayfeld improvised a little,
    simple, two-note tune—
first one note held, repeating liltingly
    upon a softer, quicker note—
which his true ears alone would understand
    sounded the cadence, Cyn • thi • a,
receding in the unfamiliar dawn
    of silken Maryland.

/ *Clayfeld's Son Selects His Specialty*

Still pressed for cash to pay his son's remaining
    college debts, Clayfeld agreed
to make a life-size sculpture of a gambler
    for the Phoenix Palace lobby

in Las Vegas. Clayfeld phoned his son, interning now
    at Denver Hospital, requesting
that they meet at the hotel for the unveiling
    of his statue since, despite
initial doubts, this work revived his wish for fame.
    Clayfeld portrayed a full-lipped man
with prominent cheekbones that made his eyes
    almost seem lost, and yet
darkly he stared, not downward at his spread cards
    taut in his stiff hand,
but to the left into the smoky room past where
    the dealer's face would be — as if
he'd had a glimpse of Lady Luck within the crowd,
    incarnate in a golden dress.
The hotel owner fixed his eyes on Clayfeld's hands
    during the banquet speeches praising
his new work; Clayfeld felt anger, certain he'd been
    scrutinized like that before.
His cheeks flushed red as smiling Lady Luck,
    who sat down by the hotel owner
in the second row, applauded him.
    Before he and his son
retired that night, numb with fatigue,
    Clayfeld won just enough,
when pausing by the slot machine, to pay
    for nightcaps for the two of them,
and that's when Clayfeld's son informed him:
    "Dad, I want to specialize
in gynecology." "You want to be a gyn . . .
    a gynecologist?" hot Clayfeld
hiccupped at his son, spilling his icy drink
    across the perfect crease
of his tuxedo leg. "You can conceive a human face
    inherent in a stone,"

his son replied; "I do the opposite—
    I tend each patient's body without
knowing whose soul lives in it. Three-quarters
    hydrogen and oxygen,
protein for muscle, calcium for bone, a talking
    monster water molecule
collapsing back to its component elements—
    that's really all we are."
"But, son, just staring at vaginas every day,
    you'll lose the sense of mystery
in human love; you'll lose the sense of *who*
    gave birth or *who* has died
when her or his dumb body dies." "Pain must be faced.
    Dad, all I want to do is help ease
anybody—no one in particular
    into the world or out.
We're only weeping water passing through."
    Fresh snow had fallen in the Rockies
all that night. Returning home at noon,
    and blankly nodding, gazing
from the window of his plane, Clayfeld could see
    some thirty gleaming miles north
to where the tilting sky sloped down to meet
    the glowing peaks, their crystal white
so inwardly intensified to blue,
    it looked as if the whole
receding mountain range were ice, and yet
    it seemed to shudder as if,
deep inside, like a volcano, it was burning, too.
    And dozing, Clayfeld dreamed
he was a child: the hotel owner sat there
    facing him; behind, his grandfather
placed his thick hand upon his shoulder as if
    once again the two of them

were strolling through his aisles of cherry trees.
    A slot machine loomed over him;
with both hands Clayfeld pulled the giant lever down
    as wheels whirled with the rasp
of cresting waves collapsing on the shore
    until, in turn, the slowed wheels clicked
abruptly into place: in the first slot—
    a cherry cluster; then, an owl—
a limp mouse dangling from its beak; and then,
    no, not another owl, though much
like one, but radiant in gold and scarlet plumes—
    a phoenix on its flaming nest.
When Clayfeld pulled the lever down again,
    three phoenixes descended
in a row, and printed coins, like tiny suns,
    flowed from an opening
as when Zeus came to Danae in a shower. "Oh!
    no one believes at heart
in his own death," moaned Clayfeld's grandfather;
    the hotel manager replied:
"I diagnose the child's obsession as a case
    of phoenix envy."—"Fraud!"
Clayfeld exploded, pushing him away,
    "Fraud! Fraud!" until the stewardess
had coaxed him back from sleep to his embarrassed self.
    And, blushing, Clayfeld looked out
at the fields of corn, as yet unharvested,
    immaculate from his plane's height,
the vast, undifferentiated, sunlit green,
    so luminous it seemed
as if this, too, were snow, as if the whole world
    were dissolving into white.
Exhausted Clayfeld dozed off once again:
    and now he saw his son,

wearing his doctor's gown, stare out into the sea
    of crescent moonlight, flickered
on the humming water crests, subsiding
    as they smoothed down hissing
softly on the shore. And still his son stared out
    in Clayfeld's restless dream,
and yet still farther out — far out to where
    it didn't seem to matter whether
anything besides the normal dark was there.

/ Mima and Melly

On the third anniversary of her divorce,
    Melly, Clayfeld's grieving sister,
bumped into Clayfeld's high-school sweetheart, Mima,
    to whom Melly had loaned money,
once upon a time, when Mima needed help
    in paying the abortionist.
Melly had hoped Clayfeld would marry Mima
    after college; she admired the way
Mima resisted Clayfeld's tendency to sink
    into romantic fantasies.
His periodic nosebleeds, rather than
    conveying what a woman's
feelings might be like, just drew him back
    into his own obsessive fears
of messy death. At the museum's show of masks
    and figurines, they met
beside a squatting goddess of fertility,
    her buttock and her breasts

plumped up like harvest moons or risen bread,
    thus forming a motif of circles
with her knees, her shoulders and her head.
    They walked out, arm in arm,
to have a cocktail before going home,
    and Mima asked if Clayfeld
ever sculpted her—if something of their love
    might have survived. Mima remembered
she and Clayfeld used to lie together
    in his father's barn, sniffing
the sweet, loose hay, pecking and nibbling
    at each other's necks until
they wandered out to watch the stars and listen
    to the wind's tide in the pines.
Melly recalled how she had aided Clayfeld
    when he built the cedar pen,
in which to keep his orphaned duck, Ishmael, warm.
    And she recalled how Clayfeld
loved to tend grandfather's cherry trees;
    he'd reach into the leafy sky,
then bring the glowing cherries to his grandmother,
    piled to the brim of her
bright blue ceramic bowl, for her to pit
    and bake into a pie.
Melly confided that she now was living
    by herself and that her anger
at her husband (her ex-husband!) still prevented her
    from feeling really free.
"It started as a dream," she said, her pushing him
    into the seven-mile gorge
below the great falls at Yosemite where they
    had spent their last vacation,
but it soon became a conscious reverie:
    she'd barely hear his cry

above the thundering, yet, for an instant,
    she could see his startled hair,
his baffled face, as if imploring her
    for one more chance, his spread arms
vainly flailing on the spray-filled air.
    "I've had a fear of heights,"
Mima replied, "since Clayfeld put me on the plane
    for college in the west
to give us needed space. I've never flown again,
    but sometimes I still feel
my insides, like a baby, dropping out of me
    from the ascending plane."
"O my! O my!" abandoned Melly moaned,
    so that the customers looked up
to find out what was happening. "O, all that pain
    from momentary sweetness. O!"
They both wept, hugging tightly in a circle,
    as they parted in the rain.

/ Clayfeld Among the Quarks

*Physicists speak of the flavor of the quarks
when making the distinction between "u" and "d"
quarks. . . . Color simply refers to an intrinsic
property of the particles, just as electrical
charge and strangeness do. . . . There are other
chargelike attributes carried by elementary
particles besides the familiar electrical one . . .
called strangeness, charm, beauty, and truth.*
                                    —James S. Trefil

Clayfeld sat up in bed at 3:00 a.m.,
    put on his baseball cap,
and woke his wife. Tears, truthful and delirious,
    slid to the crevices
around his lips. "The dinosaurs are dead —
    the latest theory claims a comet
hit the earth and raised a cloud of dust so huge
    the photosynthesizing sun
could not sustain the plants they ate," dark Clayfeld said.
    "I never meant to keep
their disappearance secret," Evelyn replied
    from underneath her pillow;
"really, dear, I would have told you if
    I hadn't known you knew."
"But did you also know our sun has used up
    half its hydrogen?
In just five billion years it will burn out."
    "Sweetheart, go back to sleep,
I promise that the sun will show its face tomorrow
    when the birds greet you,
our Vermont St. Francis, at their feeding place."
    Still Clayfeld couldn't rest:
"We've got to figure out how much material
    the universe contains —
it's like the question whether God exists —
    for if there's mass enough,
someday the stars will hurtle back,
    the *red shift* will reverse to blue,
and finally all matter will implode
    in one *big crunch* just like
the *big bang* fifteen billion years before,
    and start the universe anew.
I grieve to think of galaxies forever
    thinning out until there's nothing

/ 90

but undifferentiated radiation
    without force to charm
chance into brewing up the soup of life."
    Yet Evelyn fed Clayfeld
bacon in the morning, cheerful, though complaining fat
    would cause his long-expected
heart attack. But Clayfeld persevered, the flavor
    of the smoky salt inspired
his tongue to savor all the spice
    of cherishing his death as if
mortality had been *his* choice, although
    the strangeness of familiar fear
returned when evening snowfall blurred all color,
    whitening the air.
So Clayfeld called his bachelor brother
    in Los Angeles, a physicist
whose work on quarks had helped trace back
    the cosmic clock to right
within a millisecond of the *big bang* that
    for Clayfeld meant: *Let there be light!*
"No one has seen a quark," his brother said;
    "they're particles deduced
from how atomic matter first evolved.
    I'll visit you in May,
and I'll explain why physicists hypothesize
    the quarks with quirky names."
He didn't come, but on that day commemorating
    Clayfeld's having joined the vast,
spectacular parade to cosmic nothingness
    exactly fifty years ago,
a box arrived marked: HANDLE QUARKS WITH CARE!
    When Clayfeld yanked the cord,
he saw six sewn, blue, beatific smiles —
    that seemed to know of earth

all that one needs to know—on six white dolls
        his brother must have made
which, Evelyn remarked, resembled plump amoebae
        linked together arm in arm.
Each wore a necklace that spelled out its name:
        first TRUTH and BEAUTY, then came
FLAVOR, COLOR, STRANGENESS, CHARM.

/ Clayfeld's Anniversary Song

*When the evolutionary biologist J. B. S.
Haldane was asked about the nature of
the creator, he replied: "An inordinate
fondness for beetles!"*

There's no accounting for
one's taste in love, my dear, even with God.
        Some 85 percent
of all animal species comprise insects,
        with an inscrutable
preponderance of beetles! Although they seem
        grotesque to you and me
(stag males can kill with their huge mandibles
        or seize their choiceless mates)
yet there they are, Nature's elect display,
        with such variety
embellishing a single theme great Bach's
        imagination pales
by comparison. Having invaded
        on water, land, and air,

adorers of decay, some woo their mates
    by rubbing their own wings
to rough out strains of ragged melody,
    while some display their fire
(protected by an inner layer of cells
    so they won't burn themselves)
delighting in each other with abandon
    we can't emulate.
A quibble in the cosmic scheme of things,
    no doubt: Nature is not
concerned with individuals, even
    species are cast away —
tonnage of dinosaurs with just a little
    climate shift. Yet, life alone
is what God seems to care about — only
    ongoing life, trying
new forms for His vast, slapdash enterprise
    of changing things. Against
such precedent divine, what arrogance
    is human constancy —
rebellion in the most unnatural
    and prideful way of love
seeking to preserve the past. No wonder
    we're appalled by death,
ashamed of our own sweat, and endlessly
    examining ourselves.
What parents ever wished their child would be
    an evolutionary
breakthrough, rendering us obsolete?
    The quintessential prayer
that dwells in every human heart repeats:
    O Lord, keep things the same;
let me be me again in paradise,
    reading in my old chair

or strolling through a grove of evergreens.
        I fear that we'll be viewed
by Him as undeserving of the life
        we've got, and punished, yet
no differently than other creatures are—
        we'll be forgotten too,
beetles and all. Who knows—perhaps someday
        He'll tire: "Enough!" He'll cry,
and start a list of everything He's done.
        And when He gets way back
to counting us, and pictures you again,
        just as I see you now—
watering the wilted fuscia hanging
        beside the limestone wall,
plucking the dead leaves from the zinnias—
        He'll think: "It's not their fault
they measured time in anniversaries
        as if their need for meaning
made me manifest in *their* intent;
        I burdened them with an
excessive will to live. But by my beard,
        my beetles were magnificent!"

/ Clayfeld's Will

        Clayfeld's twin brother died
from one quick stroke while making love; he left
        Clayfeld the microscope Clayfeld
had given him when they were groping boys,
        with this departing note:
"To earth, laid well to rest, all lovers come;

I'd rather writhe in pundemonium."
    Clayfeld could picture, as if
yesterday, how he had watched the plump amoeba
    stretch itself until it snapped
and *presto*—where one was there now were two.
    Now with his brother gone,
he realized composing his own will
    was overdue, and though ideas
of "afterlife," except as particles like quarks,
    had always seemed absurd to him,
yet his decision to be buried with mementos
    eased his grief, distracted with
the teasing that he took from Evelyn.
    "Maybe a thousand years from now,
my dear, after our blasted world has cooled,
    some archaeologist from Mars
will excavate my grave and resurrect
    the story of my life."
So Clayfeld specified his casket must
    be made of lead, then he
enumerated everything selected
    to be sealed within:
his microscope, his baseball bat and glove,
    his sculptor's tools, his pruning shears,
his wedding ring etched with bright birds in flight,
    his two-note hunting horn,
the six quark dolls (his brother's birthday gift to him)
    beaming their sewn blue smiles,
his recipe for chicken soup engraved on brass,
    his inlaid riddle box,
his son's toy stethoscope, four miniature studies
    he had made for full-scale statues—
one of Ishmael, his duck, another, Buff,
    the family's recurring dog,

a bust of Freud before the cancer locked
 his resignation in,
Don Giovanni strumming on his mandolin.
 Clayfeld flew to New York
to sign the will where his old college buddy's
 female partner greeted him.
Because most everyone he met these days
 appeared familiar, Clayfeld
didn't mention he suspected he had met
 Ms. Marigold before, and surely
this was not the proper time to flirt. Hazed air
 hung still with sooty heat,
the office air conditioner was on the blink,
 and, standing by the window,
blotting the light trickle from his nosebleed,
 Clayfeld watched the traffic
back up twenty blocks, complaining, "For the sake
 of human scale, buildings
should not reach higher than the highest trees."
 Ms. Marigold walked up behind him,
put her hands upon his shoulder blades,
 and Clayfeld instantly recalled
the first, familiar lightness of that touch —
 Mima, of course, it was
Mima's deliberate, hoarse, high-school voice:
 "I never could have children
after what we did." And there they were again
 in the white waiting room
of the abortionist. His arms spread out
 to catch himself as in his dream,
Clayfeld fell toward the pond within the square below
 beside the benches where he thought
he saw his brother opening a newspaper.
 He watched his helpless shadow

warping in the windows going past; he saw
    gulls glisten in the pattern
of their scattered flight; the mayor of New York,
    he thought, would purchase for the park
his still unfinished statue of himself as he casts
    bread crumbs on the water:
CLAYFELD OF THE DUCKS his epitaph would say,
    commemorating for the citizens
that an important sculptor once dropped by
    to touch their blue lives on his way.
A tear—perhaps caused by the dusty wind—
    emerged from Clayfeld's eye;
his last thought was: he didn't have his baseball cap
    to wave good-bye.

/ Narrator's Epilogue

Reader, forgive me, but I'm not sure
Clayfeld's being shoved out of a lawyer's window
    by a willful woman is
a suitable conclusion for his life,
    despite his dreams of falling
which continued from his childhood. Frightened dreams
    hardly distinguish him even
from his own twin. His death ought to express
    some quintessential quality
that made his life distinct. With murder only
    feigning in his heart,
the ancient law of talion is fulfilled
    without an interrupting death

by human hands, merely by nature's course
    from gradual old age, or,
like his father and his brother, from a stroke,
    since all indulged in spicy foods.
Maybe I'm still not ready to let Clayfeld go
    and double back to my
surviving life. His chest and shoulders ache
    from splitting wood; his pulse rate
is too high, but basically his health is good;
    he'd love to have some grandchildren,
outlive his rivals at the university, though,
    most of all, his mind still thrills
to images of roughhewn marble not yet
    smoothed to living shape.
That block with branching rivulets of blue
    might well release sweet Evelyn
about to bathe; and *this* block, delicately
    ribbed with gray, could be
a snowy owl having come from Canada
    to perch at dawn in Clayfeld's hemlock—
or a phoenix stirring from five hundred years of sleep,
    its fabled wings spread stiffly,
ready now to mount the blast of circling wind.
    Shall we agree to one last lark,
dear reader, since it's no less plausible that Mima,
    overjoyed at seeing Clayfeld
once again, would kiss him wetly on the lips,
    reverting for an instant
to the girl she was? Why not? The office radio
    plays *La Bohème*; *"Senza rancor,"*
the blissfully heartbroken tenor sings
    as Mima lingers on their kiss,
then snatches from her purse a picture of her son
    with promise in his eyes.

/ *98*

An upsurge of relief sweeps Clayfeld from the room,
    into the plane, and home once more
to harvest in Vermont where perfumed Evelyn, bemused,
    arising rosy from her bath,
like Venus dripping spellbound from the sea, opens
    their great oak door to cello swells
and welcomes him. Out of the wheeling swirl of stars,
    the pulsing of the northern lights
that shed their aura faintly on his hair,
    arousing Clayfeld steps into
his house as Evelyn exclaims: "Are you aware
    that you forgot to pack
your baseball cap? Without its charmed protection, thank
    the laughter of our fabulous creator,
O my love, it now appears *I have you back.*"

Clayfeld Rejoices,
Clayfeld Laments

was set in Galliard by Crane Typesetting, West Barnstable, Massachusetts. Designed by Matthew Carter and introduced in 1978 by the Mergenthaler Linotype Company, Galliard is based on a type made by Robert Granjon in the sixteenth century, and is the first of its genre to be designed exclusively for phototypesetting. A type of solid weight, Galliard possesses the authentic sparkle that is lacking in the current Garamonds. The italic is particularly felicitous and reaches back to the feeling of the chancery style, from which Claude Garamond in his italic had departed.

The book was designed by Virginia Evans. It has been printed and bound by Haddon Craftsmen, Scranton, Pennsylvania.